ETHNIC
L.A.

Bradley International Terminal,
Los Angeles International Airport

ETHNIC
L.A.

Zena Pearlstone

Hillcrest Press

Copyright © 1990 Hillcrest Press
All rights reserved
Library of Congress No. 89-082027
ISBN 0-914589-05-9
Printed in Japan

HP

Hillcrest Press
Post Office Box 10636
Beverly Hills CA 90210

Contents

The city of Los Angeles has always presented peculiar difficulties to the analyst. Over a period of several decades, Los Angeles has probably been the most rapidly changing urban center in the Western Hemisphere. Between 1870 and 1940, the city grew from a dusty cow-town with 5,728 inhabitants to a teeming metropolis with a population of 1,504,277.
— Earl Hanson and Paul Beckett, *Los Angeles: Its People and its Homes,* Los Angeles: The Haynes Foundation, 1944:2.

Every city has its boom, but the history of Los Angeles is the history of its booms . . . . Other American cities have gone through a boom phase and then entered upon a period of normal growth. But Los Angeles has always been a boom town, chronically unable to consolidate its gains or to integrate its new population.
— Carey McWilliams, *Southern California: An Island on the Land,* Salt Lake City: Peregrine Smith, 1983:114. First published 1946.

We are witnessing a transformation of the Los Angeles basin into the first continental, multiracial and multiethnic metropolis in the U.S., that is, where whites are no longer the predominant majority.
— Kevin McCarthy, Rand Corporation Demographer, *Wall Street Journal,* January 15, 1985.

Los Angeles . . . may truly be the first twenty-first century city/region in America. It is neither one center nor one city, neither one dominant group nor one identity, but a spellbinding diversity most truly representative of what the nation is today and will become tomorrow.
— Elliot R. Barkan, in *Freedom's Doors: Immigrant Ports of Entry to the United States,* Philadelphia: The Balch Institute, 1986:90.

No community has lived with so many different groups in one area before. New York and London come close, but Los Angeles is first.
— Los Angeles Department of Health Services Report, September 1989.

In 1989, Los Angeles County was estimated to be: White, 41.9 percent; Hispanic, 35 percent; Black, 11.3 percent; Asian/Pacific, 11.8 percent. (Other is about .5 percent.)

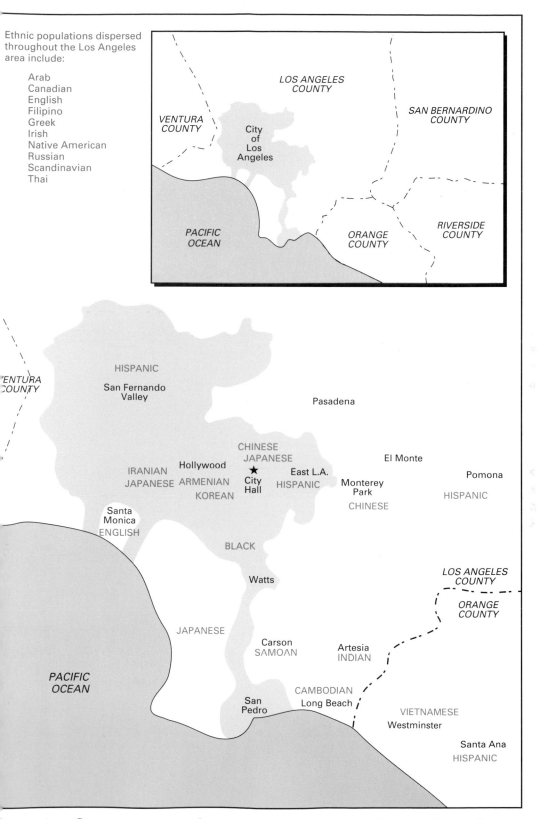

Ethnic populations dispersed throughout the Los Angeles area include:

Arab
Canadian
English
Filipino
Greek
Irish
Native American
Russian
Scandinavian
Thai

LOS ANGELES COUNTY

VENTURA COUNTY

SAN BERNARDINO COUNTY

City of Los Angeles

PACIFIC OCEAN

ORANGE COUNTY

RIVERSIDE COUNTY

HISPANIC

San Fernando Valley

Pasadena

VENTURA COUNTY

CHINESE
JAPANESE

El Monte

Pomona

IRANIAN
JAPANESE

Hollywood
ARMENIAN

East L.A.
HISPANIC

KOREAN

City Hall

Monterey Park

HISPANIC

CHINESE

Santa Monica
ENGLISH

BLACK

Watts

LOS ANGELES COUNTY

ORANGE COUNTY

JAPANESE

Carson
SAMOAN

Artesia
INDIAN

PACIFIC OCEAN

San Pedro

CAMBODIAN
Long Beach

VIETNAMESE
Westminster

Santa Ana
HISPANIC

:thnic Concentrations in the Los Angeles Area

For Arnold

Who knew that heaven was anyplace that had as many
Indian, Japanese, Afghani, Moroccan, Cuban, Korean
and Middle Eastern restaurants as Los Angeles

Foreword

This book describes the mosaic of ethnic peoples and cultures that is Los Angeles. For those groups which have a substantial history in the area—particularly the Mexicans, Chinese and Japanese who have been here for more than a hundred years—I have briefly traced their history and the ways in which their place in the city has changed over time. For the many groups who have been arriving in significant numbers since the 1960s or 1980s I have indicated, whenever possible, why they came and how they have adapted. In all cases an attempt has been made to treat each people as the independent group that they are, and I hope that their view of Los Angeles and the United States has been conveyed rather than my own. Clearly, however, in the interests of space and in some cases because of insufficient available information, there are peoples who, though they deserve to be discussed individually, have been treated as part of a group. It should not be assumed that they are considered to have made fewer or less important contributions to the area.

In the same vein ethnic populations are seldom in themselves homogeneous; in many cases there are members of an ethnic group who have lived in Los Angeles for generations while others are newcomers to the area. Distinctions between these subgroups are often hazy and appropriate terminolgy is lacking. At which generation, for example, does one stop being a Japanese-American or a German-American and become simply an American? I suspect, in addition, that the definitions of such distinctions are not consistent for all groups. For some peoples the number of subgroups, if acknowledged, would be unwieldy; for those like the Japanese, Europeans and Canadians there are citizens in the home country making decisions about events in Los Angeles, citizens living here temporarily or permanently, those who have become United States citizens, members of the second, third and fourth generations and so on. If such distinctions are applicable, I have tried to make clear which categories of a group are being discussed.

This book by its nature must necessarily harbor a certain amount of inconsistency; there is simply not the same amount or the same kinds of information available for all groups, nor do all groups lend themselves to discussion under the same categories. Available information depends on how long a people have been here, how many there are, how easy or difficult it has been for them to adapt economically and socially, and how conscientiously their activities have been followed by scholars and the media. Certainly those peoples who appear "more foreign" and those who are here in greater numbers tend to get more "press." Europeans and English-speaking peoples (like Australians and Canadians), whose cultures tend to allow them to assimilate fairly easily into American society, are seldom discussed by the media as local ethnic communities.

Population figures are particularly difficult to reconcile and all cited here must be considered as relative. There are several problems involved. The figures from the 1980 census are by now severely out of date, and the numbers that circulate in the press are generally estimates from the groups themselves and may be inflated or deflated depending on the circumstances. Immigrants here illegally are counted when they can be found but hundreds of thousands are missed (some think there are as many as two to three million undocumented residents in California). Sources often do not indicate whether they are estimating numbers for the city, county or metropolitan region, each of which is an extremely different geographical area. The City of Los Angeles occupies only 465 square miles and shares the County with 84 other independent cities. Increasingly the term "Los Angeles" is coming to refer to the metropolitan area encompassing at least parts of five different counties (Los Angeles, Orange, Riverside, San Bernardino and Ventura), 150 different cities and municipalities, more than 18 business and retail centers with an area of 34,000 square miles (of which the City of Los Angeles comprises about two percent) and a population of almost 13½ million.

Cultural diversity has long been one of my own primary interests; one that prompted me, some twenty years ago, to begin graduate studies in Native American art history. Chance and good fortune landed me in Los Angeles. When the idea for this book was proposed in late 1986, I saw an opportunity to mesh my interest in "the other" with my ever-increasing fascination with Los Angeles. Some of us had become more and more aware of both the exquisite diversity of peoples in the Los Angeles area and the need for a readable book delineating background and information about these groups.

I have tried to keep the book as current as possible, but as the status and circumstances of immigrants, in particular, change daily there are bound to be some facts and issues which are out of date as soon as the book goes to print. This study, however, has always been intended to be more than just a series of facts, and my primary hope is that the feelings and voices of the peoples who comprise today's Los Angeles are heard. This is their book.

Zena Pearlstone
Los Angeles

FOREWORD

Hsi Lai Temple (detail), Hacienda Heights

Preface

The peoples of Los Angeles—Hispanics, Asians, Europeans, Middle Easterners and Africans—come alive in this readable and informative book, a cross between a guided tour and a historical journey which delights in the ethnic diversity of our city.

Angelenos in search of fuller understanding and enjoyment of our communities will find it invaluable for its descriptions of festivals, ethnic communities and cultural resources and for its revealing look at the history of the city since its founding in 1781. All Americans will find this an important book because what is happening now in Los Angeles will increasingly occur across the country.

Los Angeles is today on the cutting edge of the twenty-first century as a result of the waves of migration which have brought diverse peoples into the Los Angeles area in the last 25 years. In the nineteenth century, European immigrants fleeing wars, famines and lack of economic opportunity poured into New York and other Eastern cities and made their way in the Industrial Revolution. In the late twentieth century, Asian and Latin immigrants fleeing wars, famines and lack of economic opportunity are arriving in Los Angeles in record numbers and struggling to find a place in the Electronic Revolution. And Los Angeles' immigrants, because of the climate and the sprawling nature of the area, seem more visible than those in the East. Ethnic variety is celebrated from the small items that people place in their windows or on their front lawns to large architectural monuments.

As Pearlstone notes, Los Angeles has always been a city of immigrants. Now, however, the newest waves are arriving at a time when the city itself is rapidly changing. How we approach these changes, whether we can celebrate our diversity and learn from one another, will influence our ability as a nation to maintain productive relationships with other countries and will also influence our quality of life at home.

The Los Angeles local economy, like that of many large cities, relies increasingly on services rather than manufacturing, but many—although certainly not all—recent immigrants are not equipped for occupations associated with international finance or the electronic and space industries. The school system which has traditionally served as a major tool for improving economic and social position today faces a monumental task serving children and adults who speak more than 90 languages.

This recent dramatic escalation of the level of diversity raises all sorts of questions for those of us who govern, work, live or visit here. This book is an important source for all. Elected officials are under constant pressure to respond to those who vote for them. This means that they are easily tempted into myopia, seeing clearly only those issues in their own districts. Like a good pair of glasses, this book makes it possible to see across town as well. For those in government and social services, it provides the kind of understanding essential to smooth operation of the city and building for the future. For those who plan to do business here, it offers the background to understand market needs and demands.

For me, however, this book is most important as an antidote to the common fear of the unfamiliar. The story it tells reveals some of the past and some of the present and often hints at the future. Yet it does so in a way that makes us long to visit the festivals, eat in ethnic restaurants and savor the variety of our community. The book is full of clues to the fun and excitement that is available in all our backyards.

I am partial to American blues, African music, Japanese restaurants, Hmong embroidery, and my Mexican neighbors. Whatever your preferences, this volume will enlarge your options.

But this is not a textbook; it is a menu.

Bon Appetit!

Ruth Galanter
Los Angeles City Council

Acknowledgements

Many people in Los Angeles have contributed to this book, some unaware that they have played a role. They include those at embassies, consulates, government agencies, social service organizations, private clubs and community organizations, who almost always enthusiastically answered my questions and unearthed information. They also include friends, friends of friends, referrals of friends, students and others who found the time to talk to me about "their people." And they certainly include the many Los Angeles *Times* and Los Angeles *Herald Examiner* reporters who inadvertently did much of my leg work. I have unashamedly devoured their words and used their reports. Their names and their contributions are listed in the bibliography. To my editor, Joyce Boss, a special word of thanks for her careful expertise and her contributions.

Ruth Galanter patiently explained to me the workings of city politics, and was always willing to share her extensive knowledge of Los Angeles and its people. Her insights have broadened my understanding of the area and the scope of this volume.

Jay T. Last first proposed the idea for this book in 1986 and our discussions over the years have shaped the final product. His ideas and practical contributions lie on each page. His warmth and wisdom are evident throughout.

Z.P.

Los Angeles Business Signs

Introduction

About two hundred years ago, what is today Los Angeles was unspoilt wilderness populated only by small Native American communities. The first immigrants—44 in number—arrived in 1781, but for the first one hundred years of its existence the town remained small and of little consequence to the rest of the country.

Population booms (one in the 1880s, a second during the 1920s, and another after the Second World War) catapulted Los Angeles out of backwater obscurity and into view as a major city. With the change in the immigration laws of the 1960s, Los Angeles became one of the most important immigrant centers in the world. A city today noted for its color, drama and offbeat qualities, Los Angeles can now claim a history, which, although short, lacks neither diversity nor interest.

In 1781, when 11 families left the town of Alamos in Sonora, Mexico, ordered by the Spanish government to come to what is now Los Angeles to establish an agricultural settlement, the Spanish authorities hoped this settlement would decrease colonial Spanish dependence on Mexico's interior and help consolidate Spanish control of California. These pioneering immigrants founded the city of El Puebla de Nuestra Senora la Reina de Los Angeles de Porciuncula (The Town of Our Lady the Queen of the Angels of Porciuncula) at the Native American village of Yang-na.*

The ethnic diversity of today's Los Angeles was foreshadowed by this Alamos group. Of the 44 individuals (22 adults and 22 children) who

---

*Yang-na was probably close to present-day City Hall. Within 50 years of the founding of the Pueblo the decimated Native American population was crowded into a ghetto near the corner of Commercial and Alameda Streets. Yang-na was one of 25 to 30 native villages scattered throughout Los Angeles County and probably had between 300 and 2,000 inhabitants. In June 1988 today's Gabrielinos, the local Native American people, protested a huge proposed development in Marina del Rey arguing that it would desecrate an ancient Yang-na cemetery.

first settled the area, eight were Native Mexican, 15 were Black and 21 were of mixed blood. Many of these original settlers are known by name. The eldest was Basilio Rosas, a 67-year-old native Mexican whose son José Carlos married a Yang-na native. Pablo Rodriguez was a farmer who was short, stocky and the father of four children. Doña Eulalia Perez taught cooking, sewing and weaving at the San Gabriel Mission,† became its *mayor domo* and keeper of the keys, and was buried there.

By 1800, the non-Native American population of Los Angeles had risen from 44 to 315, and until 1848 Southern California was peopled by Native Americans, Mexicans and the Spanish *"gente de razon"* (the priviledged class). The first of a stream of American and European adventurers who arrived in the area was José Antonio Rocha, who came from Portugal in 1815 and built himself an ostentatious home which later served as the first city hall. Rocha was followed by one Joseph Chapman, known as "José el Ingles" from Philadelphia or Boston. Chapman was a young Yankee sailor on what was most likely a pirate ship who, because of transgressions at sea, was given into the custody of the Natives in Los Angeles in 1818. There was also a Black pirate, Thomas Fisher, of whom there is no further record. These two remained the only foreign residents until the overland parties began arriving in 1826. From that date on, the locals were joined by other colorful American, British, Scots, German and French adventurers who drifted into Southern California. According to McWilliams:

> These curiously assorted individuals became naturalized citizens of Mexico, joined the Catholic Church, and married daughters of the *gente de razon* . . . Hispanicizing their surnames, they adopted the prevailing speech and style of dress. Eager to become identified with Spanish upper-crust, they assumed the forms of Spanish culture with cheerful alacrity.

When the Spanish settlement became a Mexican provincial capital in 1822 the change was imperceptible to the natives who, McWilliams notes, "dutifully changed the flag flying over the Plaza, replacing the Spanish lion with the Mexican serpent." On January 21, 1836, Los Angeles' status was elevated from *pueblo* (town) to *ciudad* (city). The serpent flew for 26 years until 1848, when California became part of the United States.

---

†The two Los Angeles Missions, San Gabriel Arcangel and San Fernando Rey de Espana, were founded in 1771 and 1797 respectively. All of the Spanish Missions were established on Native American village sites—that is, where Native Americans lived in greatest numbers; the village of Yang-na became Los Angeles.

In 1850 there were 3,530 people in the Los Angeles area. The first official census in 1860 recorded 11,333 in Los Angeles County.§ The City, in one of the several population inversions that came to characterize Southern California, was populated by Europeans before Americans. Following the initial group of adventurers and before the arrival of the midwesterners beginning in the 1880s, a variety of European groups appeared on the scene. McWilliams describes these immigrants as "exotic Polish intellectuals, British remittance men, Chinese immigrants, Basque sheep-herders, French and German peasants, and German-Jewish merchants and financiers."

These foreigners helped transform the small, sleepy mission outpost, engaged mainly in cattle ranching, into a tough frontier town which retained a distinct Mexican ambience even after gaining independence from Mexico. The mood of the town changed in the 1880s when, with the completion of the transcontinental railroads, Americans, mainly midwesterners, began to find their way west.‡ But Los Angeles was never a Mexican city, and certainly never a Mexican city that was taken over by Whites. What made Los Angeles a city was the late nineteenth-century flood of midwesterners. The population of Los Angeles County increased nearly 250 percent between 1880 and 1890, from 33,000 residents to 115,000.

The influx of midwesterners was, in part, a response to the reactions of visitors and promoters. From the middle of the nineteenth century on, visitors praised the climate, the new "frontier," the availability of enormous tracts of land which, though somewhat dry, had the potential for high fertility. Those who stood to gain from an increase of tourists and settlers—land developers and those with railroad interests—extolled the virtues of Southern California's weather and geography. On the scene, however, life was not so rosy. During the 1860s and early 70s racial friction surfaced in various ways; angry Whites turned on the Chinese, and *bandito* activity was prevalent. Smallpox raged. In 1877 drought destroyed the sheep and cattle industry. Benjamin Wilson, an Angeleno of the time, reacted to depressed real estate and cattle prices by writing that he had "never seen Los Angeles so bad. What's in store for her, God only knows. If there was anywhere to go, I would delight

§In 1851 Los Angeles County stretched from the Tehachapi Mountains on the north to San Juan Capistrano on the south and eastward to the Colorado River. Decreases in the county's area in 1853, 1865 and 1889 reduced the county to its present 4,000 square miles.

‡In 1869 the transcontinental railroad was completed to San Francisco; the extension to Los Angeles was completed in 1876. The Santa Fe Line, a direct line from the East, was finished in 1886.

to leave." Bankruptcy and foreclosure led to the subdivision of the great *ranchos* and this in turn fed the growing desire for land; small-scale agriculture replaced ranching as the primary livelihood.

The diverse nature of the city as we know it today had its beginnings in the 1870s. At the same time as the midwestern colonies were forming—Pasadena, for example, founded in 1873, was originally known as the 'Indiana Colony'*—Sir George Simpson of the Hudson's Bay Company described Los Angeles as that "noted abode of the lowest drunkards and gamblers." After 1880 the Hispanic element was almost totally eclipsed as American migrants poured into Southern California. Unlike other large American cities which grew in the nineteenth century through European immigration, Los Angeles absorbed newcomers primarily from the north-central states, a trend that continued through the first three decades of the twentieth century. Increasingly these were people of modest means who came west to retire and were described by Charles Fletcher Lummis as:

> the least heroic migration, but the most judicious; the least impulsive but the most reasonable. In fact, they were, by and large, the most comfortable immigrants, financially, in history. Instead of Shanks Mare, or prairie schooner, or reeking steerage, they came on palatial trains; instead of cabins, they put up beautiful homes; instead of gophering for gold, they planted gold—and it came up in ten-fold harvest.

Later American settlers came because of the oil and movie industries, both of which clothed the city in romance. In addition, the chance to earn a living in a place where jobs were being created by rapid expansion attracted tens of thousands. Water diverted from the Owens Valley and the Colorado River permitted a large city to grow in what is essentially a desert climate. Los Angeles never was a city by the ocean—it was founded and it expanded 15 to 20 miles inland. (Going to the beach was an excursion which could take several days and waterfront property was not premium until the 1970s.) Oceanfront real estate began to rise when water piped in from the Owens Valley made more land available. Finally, the completion of the Santa Monica Freeway in the mid-1960s made Santa Monica, Venice and Malibu accessible as bedroom communities, where rezoning created a building boom along the coast.

---

*Pasadena was the second major colony. The first was Compton, founded in 1867 as a Methodist Church enterprise pledged to teetotalism.

European immigration throughout the nineteenth century brought some colorful settlers. There were various pockets of French, and a colony of German settlers was established at Anaheim. The French artist Paul de Longpre traded, in 1901, three paintings of flowers for three acres of land near what is now the corner of Hollywood Boulevard and Cahuenga Avenue. The most colorful European immigrants of the time were a group of Polish intellectuals who established themselves in Anaheim (to be near the Germans) around Madame Modjeska (see page 102). This sojourn lasted only two years, after which they returned to Europe.

With the turn of the century the number and size of national and ethnic groups began to increase. The Russian, Mexican, Black, Asian and European populations expanded. Commerce and industry began, for the first time, to rival agriculture.

During the 1920s about 1,300,000 people moved into Los Angeles County, most from the midwest. The peopling of Southern California in this decade has been characterized as the largest internal migration in American history. Less than four percent of these newcomers settled on farms; most came directly to the City of Los Angeles which reported a population increase of 114 percent for the decade. The development of transcontinental automobile travel on all-weather highways had somewhat the same relation to the boom of the 'twenties that the completion of the Santa Fe railroad line had to the boom of the 'eighties.

At the same time a different group of migrants were arriving. The motion picture industry attracted, according to McWilliams:

> dwarfs, pygmies, one-eyed sailors, showpeople, misfits and 50,000 wonder-struck girls. The easy money of Hollywood drew pimps, gamblers, racketeers and confidence men. The increasing fame of Southern California lured much of the wealth of the Coolidge prosperity to the region.

By the early 1930s, John D. Weaver noted, "every other Angeleno pinching the beefsteak tomatoes at the new Farmer's Market had been living somewhere else less than five years earlier."

Los Angeles underwent an abrupt change in character in the years following World War II. Before the war the largest of the foreign-born populations were, in descending order, Mexican, Canadian, Russian, English, German, Italian and Irish. There were, in addition, substantial numbers of native-born Blacks and Asians. Comparing pre-war Los Angeles to New York, Chicago and Philadelphia, Earl Hansen and Paul Beckett noted that Los Angeles had the least number of foreign-born residents (14.3 percent compared to New York's 27.9 percent and Chicago's 19.8 percent). All of these cities had a significant Black population; what made Los Angeles unique, even at that time, were the large numbers of Mexicans and Asians. Despite these groups, however, the City was primarily a collection of midwestern villages. McWilliams vividly describes Los Angeles' midwestern imports:

> These good folks brought with them a complete stock of rural beliefs, pieties, superstitions and habits—the Middle West bed hours [which survive in the Los Angeles of today], the Middle West love of corned beef, the church bells, *Munsey's* magazine, union suits and missionary societies. They brought also a complacent and intransigent aversion to late dinners, malt liquors, grand opera and hussies. They still retain memories of the milk can, the newmown hay, the Chautauqua lectures, the plush albums, the hamlet devotions, the weekly baths.

With the war a true city began to emerge. At the beginning of the 1940s, Blacks, Asians and Mexicans, most living in the lowest rent districts, comprised a total of more than 200,000 residents in a population of about 1,500,000. More than 34,000 Asians included Japanese (the largest groups living around Sawtelle Boulevard in the western end of town and in the extreme east section of the city), Chinese, Filipinos, Koreans and Indians. There were Russian communities in East Los Angeles and in Venice. Canadians, British, Germans and Italians were dispersed throughout the city.

The war and the industry that was being generated at the time brought another tide of migrants to Los Angeles after 1940: Blacks from the Deep South, industrial workers from the Middle West and East, sharecroppers from Oklahoma and farmhands from Texas. In addition, due to readily available air travel, Los Angeles, by the end of the war, was welcoming more new immigrants from all over the world to their first home in America than any other city. Pan American Airlines began the first international flights into Los Angeles in December 1946. Thus began the invigoration of cultural diversity coupled with new social problems. Many of these new immigrants, as they shifted to a radically different culture, had more trouble assimilating than had the earlier settlers from Europe.

The 1970s saw the next major change in the population of Los Angeles. With the 1965 revision of the United States Immigration Law, which removed barriers to residents of Third World countries, the foreign-born population increased 49 percent throughout the 1970s, compared with less than ten percent for the 1960s. Before this revision 60 percent of the immigrants to the United States came from Europe; now, 80 percent were from Asia and Latin America. As these peoples became permanent residents, Los Angeles took on the character that it has today. In the course of the 1970s the Hispanic population doubled, the Asian nearly tripled and the total population increased by 1.8 million, of whom almost one third were immigrants. The flow continued in the 1980s; between 1982 and 1985 the ten immigrant groups admitted/processed in the District of Los Angeles in descending order of frequency were Vietnamese, Koreans, Chinese (from Taiwan, Hong Kong and the People's Republic of China), Filipinos, Mexicans, Iranians, Cambodians, Salvadorans, Soviets and Indians.

Today, Los Angeles has become the first multiracial and multiethnic metropolis in the continental United States—that is, where Whites are no longer the predominant majority (Honolulu is the prototype)—but according to demographer Kevin McCarthy of the Rand Corporation, the rapid growth of Los Angeles is over. While the presence of lower-skilled manufacturing and service jobs keep immigrants coming, other groups, in particular middle-class Whites, began emigrating in the mid-1980s. While affluent Whites, Mexicans, Filipinos, Koreans, Blacks, Vietnamese and other racial and ethnic groups continue to resettle, internal growth is exceeding the rate of immigration. In 1986, eight out of ten new members of the city were born here. On the other hand, had it not been for immigration—primarily from Asian and Latin American countries—Los Angeles would have lost about 250,000 residents between 1970 and 1980; instead it gained 150,000. By 1984 Whites made up less than half of the city's population and the relative size of the Black population has declined in recent years. The combined Hispanic and Asian population is on its way to becoming a majority.

Vermont Avenue Mall

Los Angeles Today

People from about 140 countries comprise the more than eight and one half million residents of Los Angeles County today. Some of these populations are substantial. Los Angeles is the second largest Mexican, Armenian, Korean, Filipino, Salvadoran and Guatemalan city in the world, the third largest Canadian city, and has the largest Japanese, Iranian, Cambodian and Gypsy communities in the United States, as well as more Samoans than American Samoa. The majority of these people have come because of the climate and the promise of economic opportunities. The city has been described as a mosaic rather than a melting pot because it is unlike turn-of-the-century New York, for example, which absorbed primarily peoples with diverse languages but with similar cultures. In today's Los Angeles many populations maintain their own identity and each has a different way of adjusting to new cultural and social patterns dependent on pre-migration values, attitudes and customs, the demographic conditions of the group in Los Angeles, and the attitudes of the existing Los Angeles population to that specific race and ethnicity and those customs. The merging of cultures and ethnic backgrounds has produced both a richness of diversity and a myriad of problems.

In December 1987, the Washington *Post*, in six major articles, examined the foreign-born population of Washington, D.C. The analyses and comments of the journalists parallel many in Los Angeles' newspapers over the past five years—both cities have noted problems concerning integration, the necessity for groups to help their own, the tension that arises between diverse groups, the problems in the school system, and similar issues—but in 1987 the foreign-born population of Washington was 12.5 percent of the total, whereas for the same year in Los Angeles it was probably well over 25 percent.* It has been reported that the Ivy

*The 1980 census indicated that the foreign-born population of Los Angeles was over 22 percent; it has increased dramatically throughout the 1980s. In 1989 the population of Los Angeles County was 41.9 percent White, 11.8 percent Asian/Pacific, 11.3 percent Black and 35 percent Hispanic.

League colleges of the East are sending recruiters to southeast Los Angeles and other minority areas of the city, as these schools come under more pressure to increase minority enrollments. The attraction here lies in the greater diversity of peoples in Los Angeles— particularly Hispanics and Asians—than there are now in East Coast communities.

Today's Angelenos can draw on the richest diversity of foods, clothing, architecture, entertainment, languages, world views, and religions available anywhere in the world. Businesses, at least for the present, have an assured supply of semiskilled labor. Ethnic groups with overseas ties are a magnet for trade and investment. In particular, Chinese, Japanese and Korean banks and heavy industries are opening branches in Los Angeles. Furthermore Hispanic businesses are more successful here than anywhere in the country.

On the other hand, peoples who arrive with no money and few skills put a drain on social and other city services. Schools, housing and health programs are overburdened. County court interpreters, for example, are needed in 80 different languages and dialects. The demand for 125 interpreters in 1975 jumped to almost 500 by 1989, and the budget from two and a half to more than six million dollars. A Rand Corporation report points out that immigrants tend to concentrate in cities, and questions whether the rest of the state will continue to pay increasing health and education costs.

The media too increasingly reflects the diverse voices of the area. KSCI Television (Channel 18) went on the air in 1977 offering foreign-language programming. Their earliest clients were Japanese and Korean. Today, it is the leading international station in the United States and broadcasts in about 13 languages including French, Arabic, Iranian, and Russian, and at least seven Asian languages. Overall the station reaches 1.7 million homes in Southern California but increasingly KSCI is becoming the voice of the Asian community. For immigrant groups the channel provides news from home countries, entertainment in their native languages and programs on how to survive in America—how not to "get taken" buying a car, for example. After the October 1, 1987 earthquake much reassurance was provided in a number of languages by KSCI. The large Hispanic population in the city supports two Spanish-language television stations and six Spanish-language radio stations. An all-Asian radio station was initiated in the fall of 1988—the first in North America—and programs on a number of radio stations are oriented to dozens of other ethnic groups.

This ethnic complexity is reflected in the printed media. According to the Los Angeles *Times* the foreign language press has grown dramatically over the past five years, moving from "a collection of mostly neighborhood weeklies offering gossip and social chatter to close to 50 internationally oriented daily, weekly and monthly journals." These newspapers and journals have begun to attract major advertising accounts, such as airlines and beer companies. The substantial Spanish audience is served by three dailies; the largest is *La Opinion* with a circulation of about 72,000. There are five daily papers competing for the Chinese market, four dailies plus four weeklies and bimonthlies for the Korean, three dailies for the Japanese and one daily and four weeklies for the Vietnamese. There are four Filipino papers, six Armenian, six Farsi, and two Indian as well as newspapers catering to Germans, French, Russians and others. Not all of these papers are financially successful. Some markets are so competitive that the papers charge low rates for advertising, and in other cases political, personal and identity needs are more important than economic issues. The question for the future is whether this foreign-language press will continue to flourish or whether more assimilated generations will turn to mainstream publications.

The Public Library system also has been changed by these new immigrants. With too little money and too little space the system attempts to keep up with expanding and mobile communities; bookmobiles have been found to be an effective way of coping in many areas. The Chinatown community in 1977 pressured the system to open a branch there, arguing that not only the Chinese in Chinatown but those in the whole metropolitan area would use the facility and thus that it could become a center for scholars and others interested in Chinese history and culture. The Library system consented to a three-year trial, during which the branch had to attain a circulation of 30,000 to keep it open beyond that time. By the end of 1987 the circulation was 340,000, and the branch has indeed become a center for Chinese studies. Little Tokyo residents have since argued for a Japanese center, and a branch was opened there in 1988.

The influx of artistic traditions and art forms led Fred Croton, general manager of the Cultural Affairs Department of the City of Los Angeles, to initiate, in 1985, the Folk Arts Program "to help promote, preserve and present the traditional artist in the city's communities" and to educate the public about the richness of the cultures in the city. The new department presented, in 1987, CityRoots, the first city-sponsored event that heralded the cultural contributions of new immigrant communities. Featured were the arts of more than 20 recently-arrived ethnic groups from Latin America, Asia and the Middle East. Thus on May 30-31 in Griffith Park some 18,000 people were treated to the likes of a Cuban orchestra, Beijing opera, Cambodian silk weaving and a Belizean fish boil-up. In the same spirit, UCLA's International Students Association sponsored in April of 1987 an "International Faire" with food, entertainment, and art exhibits from 20 countries. In Long Beach, the first annual "Long Beach Carnaval" held in May of 1988 attracted about 50,000 people and permitted any nationality to participate.

October has been designated by the Los Angeles County Commission on Human Relations as "Cultural Diversity Month." KCET-TV, one of the participating organizations, has featured programs on Los Angeles' Buddhist temple, Cambodian Dance, the Yiddish Theatre, and on many of the native countries of today's Angelenos.

Despite the energy and talents of these immigrant groups, the diverse population is not without problems. Large numbers of illegal immigrants and frighteningly increasing numbers of immigrant teens living on the streets create special areas of concern. Many who are here illegally survive by cleaning houses, driving taxicabs and working in gas stations. When asked for social security numbers, some make them up. California driver's licenses—certainly the major form of legitimacy in the state—can be obtained by showing birth certificates from foreign countries, and in Los Angeles the written exam can be taken in Spanish. With a driver's license bank loans can be obtained. Considering the demand, it is not surprising that the trade in fake documents of all kinds is booming. According to *Time* Magazine, in Los Angeles fake driver's licenses can be had for $60 to $65 and "green cards" (Alien Registration Cards) for as little as $25.

Most analysts think the tide of illegal immigrants cannot be stemmed. Lucie Cheng, head of Asian-American studies at UCLA, has said, "If you really want to do something about immigration, you improve the economies of the native countries." Some, but certainly not all, of the problem is currently being addressed with the new amnesty program for illegal immigrants. However, recently arrived refugees from various Asian and Central American countries, probably numbering in the hundreds of thousands, are not eligible for amnesty. A Rand report in 1983 predicted that 200,000 to 250,000 new immigrants would enter the state annually throughout the 1980s—most going to Los Angeles and San Francisco. The majority of these immigrants would be from Asia and Latin America and about 60 percent would be poorly educated, generally unskilled and potential heavy users of public services. In the main these predictions appear to have been correct.

While intergroup strife has, for the most part (considering the number of groups) been avoided in Los Angeles, racial tension has flared between Blacks and Koreans. Less publicized tensions have arisen between factions of ethnic groups, such as the Chinese, who are often now forced to live together in ways different than in their native countries. Friction seems inevitable when immigrant groups move into previously all-White areas; this has been true even when the immigrants have revitalized dying neighborhoods, as with the Indians in Artesia. Objections always seem to be found to the building of others' religious monuments, such as the Hindu Temple in Calabasas or the Buddhist Temple in Hacienda Heights. In these cases the protests were assuaged and these two architectural treasures have been constructed.

Much understanding and many open minds are needed to deal with the myriad of problems, ideas and world views created by the ethnic mix of present-day Los Angeles. Misunderstandings are inevitable and cultural differences must become a part of our education. Sacred fires of Native American religious groups must be viewed differently from Saturday barbecues on the beach. The different sense of time which most Hispanic and African cultures follow is unlike that of Whites, and must be appreciated. A Vietnamese curing technique, in which parents cut the skin of their children with the serrated edge of a coin, (called "coining" or *cao gio*), is a practice which is difficult for the White community not to see as child abuse. A few years ago, following the age-old customs of her culture, a Japanese woman killed her children (and tried to kill herself) after learning that her husband was having an affair, a practice known as parent-child suicide (*oyako-shinju*). If brought to court, the defendants in such cases use the "cultural defense," which argues that "someone reared in a foreign culture should not be held fully accountable for conduct that violates United States law but would be acceptable in the country or culture where he or she grew up." We all need to try to accommodate because, at least in the near future, the stream of new immigrants will not abate. In Los Angeles "minorities" already comprise more than 50 percent of the population.

Public School Children

Public Schools

Of the almost 600,000 children enrolled in the Los Angeles Unified School District (LAUSD) in 1988, more than 500,000 were non-White. (These numbers do not represent all the school-age children in the district; almost 100,000 are enrolled in private schools and many others may not be in school at all). They speak about 96 different languages. The district has the nation's largest number of limited-English-speaking students—including more than 40 percent of those entering kindergarten—and the most diverse array of languages. The following are the primary ones:

Afghan, Afrikaans, Amharic, Arabic, Armenian, Basque, Bengali, Bulgarian, Burmese, Cantonese, Ceylonese, Cherokee, Creole, Croatian, Czech, Danish, Dutch, Farsi, Filipino, Finnish, French, German, Greek, Guamanian, Gujarati, Haitian Creole, Hawaiian, Hebrew, Hindi, Hopi, Hmong, Hungarian, Ibo, Icelandic, Ilocano, Indonesian, Italian, Japanese, Javanese, Khmer, Korean, Kurdish, Lao, Latvian, Lithuanian, Malay, Mandarin, Melanesian, Navaho, Nepali, Norwegian, Pashto, Polish, Portuguese, Punjabi, Romanian, Romany, Russian, Samoan, Serbian, Serbo-Croatian, Sinhalese, Slovak, Spanish, Swahili, Swedish, Thai, Tibetan, Toishanese, Tongan, Turkish, Urdu, Vietnamese, Visayan, Yiddish and Yoruba.

At Hollywood High School, which draws on a particularly rich ethnic neighborhood, 35 languages are spoken by the immigrant students, more than 75 percent of the student body. The majority of students speak Spanish and Armenian. The other languages are English, Romanian, Farsi, Tagalog, Khmer, Lao, Samoan, Vietnamese, Thai, Afghan, Dari, Urdu, Cantonese, Portuguese, Russian, Hebrew, French, Bengali, Korean, Hungarian, Arabic, Hindi, Visayan, Formosan, Gujarati, Mandarin, Greek, Mandingo, Swedish, Polish and Tahitian.

In the Fall of 1988 more than 50 percent of the incoming students in the LAUSD were Hispanic; overall the percentages for 1988 were 59 percent Hispanic, 16.8 percent Black, 15.8 percent White, 8.2 percent Asian/Pacific Islander and .2 percent American Indian/Alaskan Native.* These percentages moreover are changing rapidly. According to one study the number of Hispanic students in the city by 1996 will increase to 64 percent and Asian students to 10 percent. Blacks on the other hand will decrease to 15 percent and Whites to 12 percent. (Percentages are of course approximate).

To better evaluate these immigrant students and to try to ease the trauma of their transition, a pilot pre-enrollment center was established in September of 1988 for the students and their families. The doctors, teachers and interpreters at the Student Guidance Assessment and Placement Center at Placencia Elementary School, which serves 35 downtown-area schools, assess the health, academic level,and language proficiency of the children and decide whether they will need special help. Some problems, like the need for eyeglasses, can be solved immediately. Everyone involved with immigrant children agrees that these services need to be offered in many parts of the metropolitan area.

The LAUSD must aggressively recruit and then train impossibly large numbers of bilingual teachers speaking about 100 different languages and dialects. In an attempt to cope with the large numbers of Spanish-speaking students, teachers are recruited from Mexico and Spain. The Mexican government has helped the school district hire a number of Mexican teachers and is hoping to send more, but Mexico does not have a teacher surplus. Samoan- and Cantonese-speaking teachers also are badly needed and attempts have been made to recruit Cantonese-speaking teachers from Vancouver. The increasing Asian enrollment has added 32 languages and dialects, including Bengali, Tongan, Gujarati and Lao and several Chinese and Filipino, to the demand for bilingual education in Los Angeles' schools. A newly-developed plan offers a $2,000 annual bonus (which may be increased to $5,000) for state-certified bilingual teachers.

Finding bilingual individuals who are willing to teach is only part of the process, as they must also be trained to teach. There are never enough of these teachers and the LAUSD is constantly trying to devise more effective bilingual programs. The $3.5 billion budget for the

*These statistics, the District Ethnic Survey Report, are obtained from teachers' classroom head counts each Fall. For comparison, the New York City Board of Education figures for 1987-88 were 20.5 percent White, 38.5 percent Black, 34 percent Hispanic, 7 percent other. In Los Angeles County, 47 percent of the 1.3 million school children are Hispanic.

1988-9 school year included, among its largest new expenditures, $19.5 million to begin new bilingual education programs and $5 million to expand the racial integration program.

Despite the School Board's increasing commitment, bilingual education continues, for some, to be a source of controversy. In 1986, California voters overwhelmingly supported Proposition 63, the English-only initiative. Arguments against bilingual education state that total immersion is the only way for students to learn English quickly and thus be able to cope in their new country, and that with so many languages at issue, it is too difficult to implement programs. Studies, however, have shown that students can learn some subjects in their native languages without hindering their progress in subjects learned in English, and that within three to six years students in bilingual programs can read and write English as well as native speakers. Just as important are the psychological factors which make the immigrant students feel less alienated and more comfortable. In addition, with the increasing interaction between world nations, the advantages of English speakers being familiar with more than one language are becoming ever more evident.

The demand for trained teachers is intensifying, since young people are not the only ones needing these services. As more non-English speakers arrive in the district, there are more adults who need and want to learn English. During the 1986-87 academic year, the LAUSD's English-as-a-Second-Language courses were attended by 208,000 adults, with somewhere between 20,000 and 40,000 on the waiting list. There are, at present, about 30 adult schools in the city.

The program for illegal immigrants, which allows them to apply for permanent residency 18 months after requesting amnesty, has sent adults back to school in droves. To be granted residency each of the one million people in Los Angeles County who applied and qualified for amnesty must either pass a citizenship test or prove that they have completed at least half of a prescribed 60-hour course in English, civics and history. After a year of planning the LAUSD in May 1988 enrolled 25,000 new students in 27 adult community schools—171,000 are expected by the end of the program. Evans Community Adult School in central Los Angeles is offering courses on a 24-hour basis. A 2 AM to 6 AM class has been added to the original 9:30 PM to 2 AM class, since the middle of the night is often the only time available for potential Americans to go to school. At 1:30 AM one Evans student, Feng Tu, a 37-year-old-Taiwanese immigrant, told a Los Angeles *Times* reporter: "I can come here now because children are sleeping. Husband is sleeping. Housework all done. Everything is OK without me."

The Los Angeles school system is committed to taking care of every child in Los Angeles—a commitment complicated by the fears and misunderstandings of recent immigrants. Some parents fear that their illegal status will bring harm to their children and therefore try to hide them from school officials. Other immigrants see the school system as a threat, an organization which violates their ethnic heritage by deliberately removing children from their place at home. Without a common language it is difficult for education officials to reassure parents (the children are often the only ones able to serve as translators) that the Board of Education is neither the Immigration and Naturalization Service nor an agency wishing to break up homes.

These immigrant students land in the arms of the school district with many problems, both physical and psychological. The children are often facing a culture and a language which are totally incomprehensible and they may at the same time be dealing with traumas of war, lost family members and relocation. To try to ease some of these problems, Newcomer Centers have been set up by the LAUSD in Crenshaw and Bel-Air which offer intensified year-long programs. During the year immigrant students practice English, get help with psychological problems and learn to deal with their new culture as they work with bilingual teachers, psychologists and counselors.

As students assimilate new problems emerge. Many live in two worlds: "When I'm in school I'm an American, but when I go home, I have to take off my shoes and be a slave," a Korean student complained to her teacher. Armenian girls rush into the bathroom on entering school to don the "American" clothes and make-up that their parents will not permit. These generation-gap problems tend to be intensified in a new country. Refugee families, in particular, may resent American culture—as one example, many are not accustomed to girls presenting themselves as individuals. They want their daughters to learn only enough English to help at home. A substantial number of students, as well as their parents, retain the fantasy that their stay in the United States is only temporary and that some day they will be able to "go home." Some students, self-conscious about using their English, withdraw into the comfort of the "home" group.

The daily problems confronted by teachers and students in the school system can seem endless. They must deal with communication and scheduling difficulties, teacher shortages, confusion in classrooms where students speak five to ten different languages and students who are traumatized or bewildered. But despite the daily hassle, the rewards can be enormous. American-born students learn daily to challenge the "priority" of their culture and absorb living history, as when five Vietnamese students at Lincoln High School in East Los Angeles revealed the pressures of their lives under North Vietnamese rule and their escape from Saigon (now Ho Chi Minh City).

In return for the wealth of knowledge about the countries and cultures these transplanted children have left behind, the personnel of the school district does its best to provide food, health services, counselling and clothing when needed. One school district official thinks that the LAUSD is second only to the United States Army in the number of meals served daily.

Los Angeles' immigrant students have initiated far-reaching changes which go beyond education. Parent-Teacher Associations whose members used to hold bake sales and admire the artwork of each other's children, now plan dental programs, collect clothing and provide support systems. Some immigrant groups, particularly those who are education-oriented, plan conferences and symposia, such as the Annual Korean Conference on Korean American Education, first held in October of 1983 to deal with the question of how immigrant groups can best be served in American classrooms.

Hispanic parents, who have often felt in the past that their children were being shortchanged in the school system, are learning through workshops in Spanish how to get their children into college-preparatory classes, how to deal with Parent-Teacher Associations, how to encourage children to do their homework and how to discipline children in an American society. Community service groups try to help parents overcome language and cultural barriers so that they can become active participants in their children's education.

Certainly planning is needed for the future. A 1986 Rand Corporation study cautions that schools will likely face a less prepared student body if the rate of immigration continues. Problems concerning curricula, health and psychological difficulties, bilingualism and rating performance among ethnic groups could become overwhelming. As well, questions of role models are beginning to arise, since it has been noted that although at present almost 60 percent of the educators are White, by the year 2000 between 70 and 85 percent of the students will be members of a minority.

The range of nationalities in the city school system is mirrored in the foreign student body of Los Angeles' universities; coming to the area as a student is often the first step in becoming a resident. In addition to the variety of American students at the University of California, Los Angeles (UCLA) in 1988 there were over 5,100 foreign students (about 15 percent of the student body) from 112 countries—with the largest numbers, in descending order, from Korea (611), Taiwan (602), Iran (511), Mexico (335), People's Republic of China (229), Canada (216), Hong Kong (200), Japan (194), Philippines (192) and Vietnam (178). These numbers are rising. A 1989 report (for all of the University of California campuses) to the University of California Board of Regents notes that over the past five years the number of freshmen has increased for all ethnic groups except Whites; Native American students increased 100 percent (115 to 230), Blacks rose by about 15 percent, Chicanos, 48 percent, Hispanics, 78 percent and Asians about 32 percent. At the University of Southern California (USC), where a greater proportion of students are non-immigrants, there were in 1987 more than 3,700 foreign students (about 13 percent of the total student population) from 109 countries with the most, in descending order, from Taiwan, Korea, Hong Kong, Indonesia, People's Republic of China, India, Saudi Arabia, Iran, Japan and Malaysia.

Business

Immigrant and foreign business in Los Angeles today runs the gamut from undocumented workers through small shop-keepers, often established in mini-malls, to the affluent foreign resident and investor buying prime real estate in many parts of the metropolitan area. Los Angeles has become a desirable target for foreign investors who see the city as having a stable economy; as one of the few big cities in the United States where expansion is still possible in terms of both available land and business opportunities. Current data indicate that Los Angeles is the nucleus of American business for Pacific Rim nations (and perhaps others) and that foreign investors are establishing a strong foothold here. In still-growing Los Angeles (as compared with San Francisco), land and real estate remain available in populated areas, including downtown, where the price of land seems relatively low to the Japanese (real estate on the Ginza in Tokyo can be as high as $25,000 a square foot and the high exchange rate on the yen in 1988 made American property even more of a "bargain") and relatively accessible to the British (in England much prime land is held in trust by established families).

Land ownership in the central city reflects the number of foreign interests here; real estate is owned by Japanese, British, West Germans, Canadians, Dutch, Israelis, Mexicans and others. Saturo Jo, a vice president with Cushman Realty, describes Los Angeles' downtown area as unique, "because it is a joint venture of both U.S. and foreign firms . . . Japanese executives see downtown Los Angeles through the same eyes as they see downtown Tokyo" which is "as a safe investment since it is in the center of activity. And from a symbolic viewpoint, Japanese, like Europeans and Middle Easterners, believe that being in the center is the mark of a leader. In ancient cities, the ruler's palace was always in the center." In 1988, according to data compiled by Cushman Realty, the Japanese owned all or part of 25 major downtown buildings, while Great Britain owned five and Canada, four.

The Japanese have been particularly active in the Los Angeles real estate market in recent years. While it is difficult to determine the precise extent of foreign investment in the Los Angeles metropolitan area, it has been determined that in 1988, for the first time, Japanese investments surpassed those of the British and Canadians. In fact, in 1988, the Japanese invested more money in Los Angeles than any other place in the country—18 percent of their total United States investment, or more than $3 billion. (Japanese call Los Angeles the 24th ward of Tokyo and claim that anything Japanese can be found in the city.) Data from the early 1980s indicates that even at that time the Los Angeles/ Long Beach area had the largest number of Asian-owned businesses in the country.

Foreign investors are not, however, limiting their purchasing to downtown areas, but the extent of foreign ownership is even more difficult to determine away from the main commercial centers; undeveloped property in particular is often bought through a third party. In July of 1989 the Los Angeles *Times* reported a possible $21.8 million sale of Marina del Rey property to unknown foreign investors. The Japanese ownership of much important real estate outside of Little Tokyo and the surrounding area underscores the impact that Japanese investment is having on the city. In addition, 70 percent of all Japanese imports enter the United States through the port of Los Angeles.

Japanese banks too are active in the area and making a strong effort to compete with California banks. Of the 12 major Japanese banks in the United States, five are in Los Angeles; at least three of California's ten largest banks are now Japanese-owned and hold more than 25 percent of California's banking business.

The Japan External Trade Organization, a semi-official, trade-promoting arm of the Japanese government, estimates that at least 1,000 Japanese corporations have opened branch offices in the Los Angeles area— probably more than 200 in 1988. Toyota, Nissan and Honda all have their United States headquarters in the Los Angeles area (as do eight other foreign automobile firms) and the JVC/Victor Company in 1989 announced a $100 million investment in a Hollywood company. The Japanese business presence in the city has become so important that the Japan External Trade Organization offers courses in Japanese-American business dealings. These courses, according to American businessmen who have flubbed Japanese deals because they did not understand the culture, are invaluable. The number of recent articles, particularly in the Los Angeles *Times*, concerning Japanese/American interactions and differences regarding management styles and business practices is yet another indication of the importance and extent of Japanese business in the city.

The Japanese business presence is also having an effect on the home real estate market. Thousands of executives of Japanese corporations are now buying rather than renting houses. As one example, a Japanese-owned firm, Haseko in 1988 built 23 high-priced condominiums in Beverly Hills, 17 of which were bought by Japanese. We should not be surprised that there are now more than 100 direct flights each week between Narita International Airport in Tokyo and Los Angeles International Airport.

While the Japanese may have the strongest Asian business presence in the city, they are far from alone. Chinese business interests are strong in Chinatown and Monterey Park and increasingly include other areas of the city. A day of trade talks with Chinese (from the People's Republic of China) and American businessmen, organized by the City of Los Angeles, was unusual in that "the members of the China Enterprise Management Association were chief executives of leading companies and governmental commissions who had the authority to make deals for specific projects." Interactions were reportedly so brisk that the staff of interpreters could not keep up with the proposals being made by the 250 American businessmen and the 40 visitors. The government of the People's Republic of China has purchased the 500-room Clark Hotel, downtown, and is remodelling the lower stories to serve as the first permanent United States outlet for Chinese imports. In 1988 Los Angeles accounted for about a quarter of the United States trade with China.

Los Angeles has also become the capital of Korean business in the United States. By 1982, 25 percent of all Korean firms in the United States were located here. The *Korean Directory of Southern California* for 1986–7 lists more than 8,000 Korean businesses in the Los Angeles area—most (according to Ivan Light) gas stations, groceries and liquor stores. As of July 1989 all 23 sunglass shops on Ocean Front Walk in Venice were Korean-owned. The *kye* system of obtaining loans (see "Asian" chapter) has been credited with much of the Korean small-business success in the city. When Koreatown Plaza opened, however, it became clear that at least part of the Korean community had moved beyond the small retail outlets that have characterized their business. Koreatown Plaza, a $25 million, trilevel indoor mall, is the biggest project undertaken by Koreans in Southern California.

The number of Hispanic-owned firms in the Los Angeles area has increased by more than 55 percent since 1982; in 1986 the Los Angeles area was home to 81 of the nation's 500 largest Hispanic businesses. A study has found 35,000 businesses in Los Angeles County owned by people with Latino surnames. The United States Hispanic Chamber of Commerce says the pace of Hispanic business expansion should continue into the 21st century, since the growth rate of Hispanic businesses is related directly to the increasing Hispanic population. While nearly two thirds of Hispanic businesses in the Los Angeles area are in the service and retail sectors, there are also a large number of Hispanic manufacturers.

With the growing number and character of foreign-born residents, Los Angeles is seeing an increasing number of both Anglo- and immigrant-owned businesses which cater to the needs—both economic and psychological—of the new inhabitants. California Center Bank in Koreatown, for example, has its employees bow and say good morning to the first customers of the day as well as administering to Korean financial habits. Korean and other banks catering to particular ethnic groups will often make loans based on cultural information or knowledge of family ties that would be unacceptable to an American bank. Observers of the Asian population, however, wonder if differences between Asian- and Anglo-Americans will continue to be notable; some feel that in about 15 to 20 years most Asians will be so assimilated that "ethnic" banks may no longer be necessary.

A Filipino immigrant who, in 1972, was unable to borrow enough money for a used car, established a large car dealership in the San Gabriel Valley where car sales are made in 50 different languages and dialects. Rather than advertise, it is left to the staff of 450—about three-quarters Asian but also including speakers of French, Arabic, Greek, Farsi and dozens of other languages—to solicit business. As at the Korean bank, the management realizes that understanding native customs is as important as understanding the language; Asians who are accustomed to buying cars from catalogues, for example, are encouraged to shop in this way. Because members of the staff are familiar with Asian culture, credit can sometimes be extended even if the buyers have no credit rating. On the other hand, the sales records of other "minority-owned" car dealerships, which do not cater to a particular ethnic group, have lagged behind ethnic population growth.

Real estate agents, too, have realized that language skills and an understanding of other cultures can make a difference. Land and real estate in Los Angeles are being purchased not only by those who have settled here but also by those who want to own land in California, and real estate companies have noted that members of immigrant groups would rather buy houses, like cars, from their own. Denis Bolen of Coldwell Banker began seeking bilingual agents in 1984. Today he has employees who speak a total of 24 languages including Spanish, Farsi, Tagalog, Romanian and Hebrew, who also have learned to cater to particular ethnic tastes; Asian buyers, for example, find American real estate tactics too aggressive and prefer a softer approach. Some real estate companies have begun advertising directly to foreign buyers. Merrill Lynch co-sponsored a live broadcast from Beverly Hills for a Tokyo audience, with some prime real estate as the attraction. With the success of that broadcast, Los Angeles realtors have been going directly to the source; a 1988 meeting was set up in Tokyo by a Japanese newspaper "in response to the enormous Japanese interest and activity in the U.S. real estate market." As a result, Joyce Rey of Rodeo Realty is looking for a Los Angeles castle for a Japanese billionaire, and other agents are hunting down office buildings and golf courses.

As opposed to the monied Japanese seeking castles and golf courses, most immigrant peoples are looking for help buying those things which are essential and expensive—homes, cars and businesses. It is not surprising that they will also look to someone familiar to help with things that may be terrifying—like learning to drive in Los Angeles. And in this car-centered culture, ethnic-oriented driving schools are thriving. It has been estimated that as many as 60 percent of Los Angeles County's 125 private driving schools are servicing immigrant groups. There are today schools catering to Koreans, Mexicans, Central Americans, Chinese, Vietnamese, Armenians, Germans, Israelis, Turks and Indians. Each group appears to have its own set of problems to overcome. Armenian instructors try to get their Lebanese students to watch the road rather than the rear-view mirror for signs of gunmen, Mexicans try to keep their students off the horn, and Asians try to help older women, who have never before sat behind the wheel of a car, from freezing with terror. Young Moon Kim capitalized on the problems he had when he first tried to get a California driver's license by trying to help others circumvent some of the aggravation and bewilderment; his driving school, now about 19 years old, caters to the Korean community. Instructors like Kim realize that they are not only teaching driving but a whole set of cultural adaptations. California police, apparently, are astonished at the number of newly-arrived Chinese who, after hours and weeks of lessons, cannot understand why they should stop for emergency vehicles.

The three million Hispanics in the city (as discussed in a following chapter) have institutions as diverse as Vons Supermarkets, Forest

Lawn Cemetery and UCLA Extension vying for their patronage. A company called L'Image Graphics has approached the Black and Hispanic markets with a new line of greeting cards. This Culver City business has been making these cards for the past five years and now has 1,500 outlets in the United States, Canada and Puerto Rico. While the company notes that the cards are designed to appeal to everyone, the people represented have brown skin tones. Available in most areas of Los Angeles the product is described by one store owner as "the only viable source for ethnic cards."

Recent immigrants who come with little money and resources have become associated with mini-malls, or "convenience shopping centers" as the developers call them; about half of these malls in Los Angeles have been started by foreign investors. Less expensive than large shopping centers or stores, the mini-mall offers relatively inexpensive start-up possibilities for small businesses, and allows immigrants to start making money in their new country. In 1987 one eight-store mini-mall at Vermont and First streets had a Filipino beauty salon, a Saudi Arabian-run butcher shop, a Cambodian doughnut shop, and a Vietnamese-run gift store, as well as a Filipino from Hong Kong renting videos and a Hispanic managing the pizza parlor. Asian entrepreneurs have been particularly attracted to these small stores; they typically put in long days and provide multiple services in their attempts to become established merchants.

As foreign interests in the area increase, more American companies in Southern California are hiring immigrants to fill professional ranks. In 1986 the Immigration and Naturalization Service (INS) issued about 70,000 visas to professionals who had been working in their native countries for companies affiliated with United States corporations and required transfers to this country—an increase of 432 percent over 1975. In addition, the INS has seen a tremendous increase in the number of foreign professionals who apply for temporary work visas that enable them to work in the United States for up to six years; these were up 250 percent in 1986 from 1975. Most of these temporary visas are issued to citizens of countries that have strong business ties with the United States—in 1986 visas to Britons were the most common followed by Canadians, Mexicans and Japanese. As applications for permanent visas have become backlogged, the demand for temporary visas has increased. Temporary visas are issued if the applicant can prove that he is a "professional" as defined by the INS and has a job in the United States. For some highly technical operations, companies bring their personnel with them. Once a temporary visa is granted, the company can immediately file for a permanent visa if they feel that they will need the employee beyond the life of the temporary one. Permanent visas are more difficult to obtain since there are annual quotas for most countries.

As the "borrowings" among old and new residents increases, Los Angeles' ethnic stores and restaurants are building their profits by capitalizing on Western and American holidays. At Christmas Asian restaurants and businesses are strung with lights and holly, and foreign-born shoppers take home seasonal gifts—both American and traditional—often for American friends rather than those of their own ethnic group. Shops in Little Tokyo do a big business in Japanese rice crackers and in Koreatown one can buy $30 silver-plated chopsticks. And in perhaps the ultimate merge, Santa Claus in Little Tokyo wears a Japanese warrior helmet.

Los Angeles City Hall

Politics

While the Los Angeles population as a whole grows more ethnically diverse, each ethnic group is itself diversifying economically and geographically. Newer immigrants tend to cluster, frequently displacing earlier immigrant groups or other minorities. The more settled groups tend gradually to disperse. Various areas of the county are changing or have changed their ethnic characteristics. Monterey Park is perhaps the most visible example where a once primarily Caucasian neighborhood is now more than 50 percent Asian. But the phenomenon is widespread—many communities in the San Gabriel Valley are substantially Asian, there are large numbers of (Asian) Indians in Artesia, Armenians in Hollywood, Samoans in Carson and Hispanics in many areas.

The questions for political leaders include how the current situation and trends effect political effectiveness, and which groups are likely to organize to strengthen their voting potential. The large (now about 35 percent) Hispanic population of the greater Los Angeles area, in particular, is becoming more vocal, better organized and more aggressive in its demands. When a high number of top City Hall jobs became vacant in 1988, the City Latino Employees Association noted in a letter to the mayor that only seven percent of the city managers were Latino and that the situation in regard to Hispanics at City Hall was getting worse. In August 1988 the Mexican American Legal Defense and Educational Fund (MALDEF) and the American Civil Liberties Union Foundation of Southern California claimed that the Board of Supervisors and other County officials discriminated against Hispanics in redrawing district lines in 1981. (A United States Justice Department suit [see below] followed on the heels of this accusation.) In September of 1988 MALDEF submitted a complaint to the State Department of Fair Employment and Housing accusing the Los Angeles Police Department (LAPD) of "discriminating against Hispanic officers in promotions and work assignments." Of the more than 7,000 personnel in the LAPD, 18 percent are Hispanic, but in top positions the percentages range between zero and seven.

In October of 1988, 300 prominent California Hispanics gathered to provide what they called a "Latino agenda for the 1990s, aimed at securing wider recognition of Latino issues." While the focal point was information rather than politics, one of the aims was to ask "successful Latinos to apply their academic, business and professional skills to achieve wider recognition of Latino concerns and political representation of Latino residents in the 1990s." (An organization called Impacto '88 has accused both Republicans and Democrats of ignoring Latinos.) The information put together in the first "Latino almanac" will help political organizers contact hundreds of Hispanic groups for upcoming political events aimed at getting more Hispanics into elected offices. But mobilizing the Hispanic community has had its difficulties, largely because many are not eligible to vote, many who are eligible do not register and many who are registered do not vote. A 1989 Washington D.C. study indicates that these traditional patterns may be changing; 81 percent of naturalized Hispanics across the country (as compared with 70 percent of all American citizens) are now registering to vote. In California, however, throughout the 1980s, Hispanics cast only six to seven percent of all votes despite the fact of a 25 percent increase in Hispanic registered voters since 1984. In addition, while 20 years ago Latinos were concentrated in certain areas of the city, today most neighborhoods tend to be ethnically mixed, as educated and successful Hispanics move out and new immigrants from other ethnic groups move in.

Hispanics, particularly Mexicans, are becoming citizens at twice the rate of a few years ago. If the rate of Hispanic applications for citizenship continues to rise, political power in Los Angeles could shift dramatically. In addition, the Federal amnesty program for undocumented residents may also significantly change the role of Hispanics in Los Angeles politics. In 1993, the first five-year amnesty period will close and the new immigrants will be eligible for citizenship; it is possible that 75 percent might apply for citizenship as soon as they are eligible.

That many new immigrants have not registered to vote, even if eligible, is hardly surprising since many of them have had little opportunity to understand how a democratic process works in practice. In many cases coming from countries where politics operates independently of the wishes of most of the community, newcomers must learn that it is possible for them to have an effect on government. For those who come knowing no or little English and without employment, becoming active in local politics is rarely a high priority.

The African-American community in the city, like the Hispanic, has experienced a lack of representation in city management positions despite the fact that there has long been a Black mayor. While about 17 percent of the city population is Black, African Americans hold only about ten percent of the city's professional and administrative jobs.

The Asian community has come to be of special interest for Los Angeles' politicians. Although it is large, now almost 12 percent of the population, it is not as politically unified as the Black community. According to a study by the California Institute of Technology, while Blacks tend to be heavily Democratic and Hispanics lean toward the Democratic party, Asians apppear evenly divided between the two major parties. Filipinos and Japanese Americans tend to vote Democratic, but the Vietnamese lean toward the Republicans, and the Chinese-American and Korean vote is divided. Whether Asians moving into Latino neighborhoods will coalesce or vote differently from their neighbors remains an open question. Asians moving into Black neighborhoods tend to cause unrest and suspicion (tensions between long-resident Blacks and new-resident Koreans have received the most media attention), which might indicate that these areas will not form a voting block.

Getting out the Asian vote, which in the past has been 10 to 11 percent lower than that of Blacks and Caucasians, is an important political concern. Asians have traditionally sought economic security through their own means and labor rather than through politics and civil rights, unlike Blacks and Hispanics who tend to make protests public and get people involved in the issues. These Asian attitudes may be changing and, if so, may have a substantial effect on city elections. The election of the first Asian American, Michael Woo, to the City Council in 1985 gave them, for the first time, a public political presence. The middle class is growing; more Asians are registering to vote, and they are becoming more heavily involved in the political process. As Asians move away from traditional incentives having to do primarily with the integrity of the family, they increasingly realize the influence that government can have on their lives.

In contrast to Western corporations, who support their own, Asian and Asian-American businesses have not traditionally helped Asian candidates; in an attempt to "Americanize" their image, they have preferred to support White candidates in the same way that they have tried to "westernize" their commercials. As the Asian community becomes more politically sophisticated, it will be interesting to note if Asian corporations will change their strategies. On the other hand, local politicians who support large-scale development can let the ethnic characteristics of neighborhoods work for them. Development in Little Tokyo, for example, is being funded primarily with Japanese money. Though this redevelopment often causes hardship for the small Japanese-American businesses, politicians can argue that the ethnic characteristic of the neighborhood is maintained.

The ethnic makeup of an area can also affect election districts which are by law drawn by population. The Federal Voting Rights Act requires that district lines be drawn so as not to divide communities. Reapportionment occurs after every decennial census or when there is a complaint of racial discrimination.

The 1990 census and perceived racial discrimination may both lead to reapportionment in the near future. Los Angeles now has a Black mayor, and the fifteen-member City Council has three Blacks, two Hispanics and one Chinese-American. The 1990 census may influence legislators to draw district lines so that Asians are more concentrated, and may indicate that the balance on the Council needs to be changed to three Hispanics and two Blacks. City districts at the present time are not suited for more ethnic appointments since a block of a single ethnic group tends not to exist in any specific district. We can anticipate, however, that after 1990 Hispanic representation will increase. Blacks are already concerned that this Hispanic representation will undermine their past gains. Other minority groups, such as Armenians, are not large enough or concentrated enough to generate a new district.

In the near future, changes are more likely to face the governing board of Los Angeles County, the Los Angeles County Board of Supervisors, than that of the City. The Board, composed of five White men, was notified by the United States Justice Department in 1988 that it was indeed in violation of the Federal Voting Rights Act by denying representation to the large Latino population in the central and eastern parts of the County as indicated by the 1980 census. This means that the County must either undertake a court fight or create a district in which a Latino candidate has a good chance of being elected. Early in 1989 Black organizers in the city entered the battle over this County reapportionment, stating that Black as well as Hispanic interests had to be considered. The Asian population, which is more scattered geographically than that of Blacks, although about numerically equal, is afraid that new district lines could further divide their neighborhoods.

There is clearly great political strength to be had if ethnic groups band together but the extent to which the various ethnic groups will coalesce is not easy to predict. The mixed-ethnic city of Monterey Park (more than 50 percent Asian, about 33 percent Hispanic) is the subject of an ongoing UCLA study which illustrates some of the difficulties inherent in understanding and predicting future trends. Researchers have found that in Monterey Park it is often difficult to understand the political processes because the changes are so rapid that data collection and analysis always lag behind the current status. City Council members Judy Chu and Betty Couch won their seats because they had support from all ethnic groups; Chu could not have won her seat without Hispanic support, and it is unlikely that any one ethnic group could ensure a candidate's election. If the present system of alliances of ethnic groups within the city continues, Monterey Park may be a harbinger of political processes in the 1990s.

Ethnic groups in other independent cities within the County, who are beginning to feel the heat of underrepresentation, may realize, like those of Monterey Park, that they will gain strength by banding together. In Culver City, for example, where, at present, all fifteen members of the three city commissions are White, members of the large ethnic minority (20 percent Latino, 11 percent Black and 10 percent Asian) are beginning to assess their political possibilities.

Some interesting coalitions which now exist and which some politicians think have real potential to change city government, are that of the Hispanic United Neighborhoods Organization (UNO) and the Black South-Central Organizing Committee (SCOC), which are not only registering voters but encouraging registered voters to sign petitions urging action on community needs. These two church-based groups representing 175,000 working class and poor families work together and more recently also with Valley Organization in Community Effort (VOICE), a mainly White group from the San Fernando Valley.

If in time second- and third-generation members of ethnic groups vote their economic and social position (or aspiring position, as the Japanese have traditionally done), rather than with their ethnic bloc, then the political future will have a different cast. Changes will occur, but they will certainly not be parallel for all groups either in kind or rate.

POLITICS

"The Plumed Serpent," East Los Angeles mural by Willie Herrón

Hispanic

Today there are about three million Hispanics in Los Angeles County (35 percent of the total population) with thousands more arriving every year; the population grew by 22 percent between 1980 and 1985, and by 2010 there may be more Hispanics than Anglos (Hispanics will out-number Whites in the City). The 1988 *Directory of the Hispanic Com-munity of the County of Los Angeles* (fourth edition) has 357 pages listing business and professional organizations. The Hispanic com-munity is visible not only because of its numbers but also because Hispanics do not assimilate readily into American culture. In 1967 Christopher Rand described them as the largest "unmeltable" group in the city, a population which chooses not to assimilate. More recently they have been called "a salad bowl..[they] mix but don't blend." Because the population is large, relatively concentrated, lives near and keeps in touch with their home countries, tends to marry other His-panics (80 percent) and continues to speak Spanish at home, Hispanics are more able than some groups to maintain their own identity.

Since 1970, Mexicans have been joined in Los Angeles by increasing numbers of Hispanics from El Salvador, Guatemala, Honduras, Nic-aragua, Cuba, Puerto Rico, Argentina, Chile and Peru. In 1988 there were students at UCLA from 23 Spanish-speaking countries. Each of these nationalities has a unique personality, and has come to the United States for differing reasons—Cubans for political freedom, Mexicans for economic gain, Salvadorans as refugees from a brutal civil war—and they quite correctly resent being lumped together as "Hispanics" (as has been done here as a convenience and because statistics on and organizations for "Hispanics" are commonly noted in media reports).

Overall, according to government statistics, more Hispanics live below the poverty line than the national average, and in Los Angeles this population is constantly fueled by immigrants arriving without jobs or resources. Partly because of these new arrivals there are continuing social problems and there is never enough affordable housing. The Los

Angeles *Times* estimated in 1987 that more than 200,000 Hispanics were living in garages, often illegally.

These social problems are compounded by the fact that Hispanics are not high education achievers, a situation which probably reflects the traditional Hispanic orientation toward support for home and family rather than the usual Euro-American (and Asian) esteem for higher education. In 1987 only about 16 percent of Los Angeles' Hispanic high school graduates had completed the University of California requirements for admission (as opposed to close to 55 percent for Asians, 32 percent for Anglos and a county average of 28.6 percent). In 1986 R. B. Valdez of the Rand Corporation profiled the present Hispanic community as largely (three quarters) of foreign stock, young (half under 18) and having a history of low educational/occupational status. In the 1980s over half the adults were foreign-born, and most noncitizens. These facts help explain the inability of the Hispanic population to translate community size into social mobility and political power.

The Hispanic community, however, is changing on various levels. Chicano studies programs on Southern California college campuses are expanding—enrollment has doubled on some campuses and classes are now drawing Anglos as well as Hispanics. In addition, universities are seeking more Chicano professors. Los Angeles has more Hispanics in business than any other city in the United States. Government statistics indicate that two percent of Hispanics hold postgraduate degrees—which would mean about 60,000 in Los Angeles County—and a growing number, men and women, are finding their way into the upper echelons of the business world. Upwardly mobile Latinos are moving into the suburbs, particularly the northeast San Fernando Valley; and as their incomes rise and they acquire property, they tend to become more politically conservative. In 1984, about 70 percent of those making over $50,000 a year voted Republican, although the working-class electorate remains largely Democratic. With two Hispanics on the City Council, and a Hispanic, Diane Pasillas, as a deputy mayor, the population is becoming more aware of what they can accomplish politically. This political power should become more apparent as an increasing number of young Hispanics reach voting age and as more Hispanics become citizens.

Today there are sizable Hispanic communities living in many areas of the county, including Alhambra, Azusa, Baldwin Park, Montebello, La Puente, Hacienda Heights, Glendale, Rosemead, Vernon, Bell, Pacoima, South Pasadena, Lincoln Heights, Boyle Heights and Eagle Rock. Spanish-language media reflects the ever-growing population.

There are three Spanish-language newspapers with large circulations: *La Opinion*, the oldest, which began in 1926 and sells more than 70,000 copies a day; *Noticias del Mundo,* the rival daily, which built up a circulation of 32,000 in only two years (and is still growing); and *El Diario*, a full-color paper launched in 1987, which achieved a circulation of about 40,000 in less than a year. These and other Spanish-language papers maintain their readership from the constant stream of Spanish speakers entering the area. The Los Angeles *Times* publishes bilingual (Spanish/English) sections which reach 419,000 "households of predominantly Hispanic population and discusses lifestyles and special events." In addition to these newspapers the city has two Spanish-language television channels (KMEX and KVEA) and six Spanish-language radio stations (KALI, KLVE-FM, KNSE, KSKQ-AM and FM, KTNQ and KWKW).

The Hispanic heritage of the city is celebrated with a "Fair for the Children"—*Feria de los Niños*—which has been held in Hollenbeck Park each June for over 15 years. Attractions include salsa and mariachi bands and folklorico dancers, and for the children there is a costume parade, face painting, piñata breaking and clown and comedy acts. As well, members of the Los Angeles City Council and the State Government are investigating possible sites in Southern California for a California State Museum of Hispanic History. Assemblyman Charles Calderon has stated that the demographics of Southern California "make a Latino museum not just desirable but essential."

In May of 1988 the first Long Beach Carnaval celebrating the Latin community of Southern California was sponsored by the Downtown Long Beach Business Associates, with hopes of enlivening the city's business center. The festivities included a parade, costumed dancers, music, craft and food booths, evening entertainment and events for children. Participation, however, was not limited to Hispanics; in 1988 there were English and Thai craft and food booths.

The growing Hispanic population has Los Angeles institutions as diverse as Forest Lawn Cemetery and Vons Supermarkets vying for the Hispanic economic market. Hispanics are creating a novel place for themselves in the city—one that does not invite total assimilation into White culture but which is not alienated from it. Vons has spent millions to create a new chain of supermarkets—Tianguis—built for and designed to attract bilingual, bicultural shoppers. Spanish-language radio station KTNQ has had an advertising campaign for a new on-air promotion—on English language television. Spanish-language advertisements are becoming big business as well. The number of Hispanic advertising firms with big-name clients such as Disneyland, Mac-Donalds and AT&T has almost doubled in the past two years. On April 26, 1987, UCLA Extension staged a "one-day celebration of Latin and South American arts and culture" to sell UCLA Extension to the Hispanic community. At the time only five percent of Extension's 100,000 students were Hispanic. Dean Leonard Freeman noted that "to a considerable extent our future as an institution is going to be affected by how many Latinos we attract." And in August of 1987, no less a Los Angeles institution than Forest Lawn unveiled "a museum and court dedicated to the past civilizations of Mexico." Ted Brandt, Forest Lawn vice-president, informed reporters that "the exhibit is . . . expected to bring more Latino visitors to Forest Lawn, and eventually, more Latino customers." As the Hispanic population continues to increase and becomes better established, it seems clear that the Hispanic market will continue to change the face of Los Angeles.

■ Mexican

Those intrepid souls from Alamos who, in 1781, overcame smallpox and desert travel on their journey from Mexico were Los Angeles' first immigrants and founding settlers. The Mexican population, however, remained small until the mass migrations between 1910 and 1930. David L. Clark notes that at the turn of the century there were only 8,000 "Mexican-born persons and their U.S.-born children" in all of California. This was "approximately one-tenth the number of Chinese in the state." By 1930 there were in Los Angeles 368,000 residents of Mexican origin.

While the percentage of Mexicans in the city has waxed and waned over the years, the Mexican presence in the Los Angeles of the 1980s ranges from the dynamic East Los Angeles murals to the ubiquitous taco. Now comprising more than 25 percent of the population, Mexicans are the largest ethnic group. Los Angeles has, in fact, the second largest Mexican population outside of Mexico City, a status it has retained since 1940. In addition, it is reputed that half of the former population of the Mexican State of Zacatecas (400,000 to 600,000) now lives in Southern California.

From 1822 to 1848, when Los Angeles was under the Mexican flag, the Mexicans in the city comprised the troops, artisans and colonists (*cholos*). These were the years of the famous *ranchos* when a strong distinction was drawn between the Mexicans and the Spanish *gente de razon* ("people of reason"), who topped the social classes. The Mexicans of this time are described by McWilliams as "a miscellaneous lot" recruited from Sonora and Sinaloa. The distinction between Mexicans and Spaniards disappeared when the *rancho* period ended and the *gente de razon* lost their money and holdings. All were now known as Mexicans. This era of Mexican sovereignty is remembered on the city seal of Los Angeles, which includes an eagle holding a serpent—a motif taken from the Mexican Coat of Arms.

After 1848, the Mexican population lived in the area just south of First Street. As their numbers increased they spread to the Plaza area which, by 1860, was known as Sonoratown, a notorious slum housing Mexicans and Chinese. In the 1870s, Boyle Heights was created east of the Los Angeles river as a Mexican community. Despite the increase in territory, however, the relative number of Mexicans decreased when California joined the Union in 1848. Possibly as a way of reinforcing the status of the shrinking community, at least ten Spanish-language newspapers were created between 1850 and 1870. These newspapers addressed questions concerning the loss of Mexican culture, decreasing Mexican political power, and increasing inequality. Racial tensions were erupting at this time although the Mexican bandito activity was much exaggerated by the English-language press.

With the great influx of primarily midwestern Americans into Southern California in the 1880s, the Hispanic element was almost eclipsed. Mexican quarters at that time were extremely localized; 88 percent lived in the *barrio*. Mexican immigration began to increase with the turn of the century, and during the 1910s large numbers arrived in Los Angeles fleeing the violence of the Mexican Revolution. They came in even larger numbers during the 1920s. The Mexican population now moved north of Third Street, near Aliso, and from there into what is now known as the Belvedere area of East Los Angeles. This move was not voluntary; developers were moving into their original community.

Olvera Street was being born. First known as Wine or Vine street (renamed to honor Augustin Olvera, the first county judge), this dirt alley in the slum had been slated to be bulldozed. At the time, however, Mrs. Christine Sterling, a woman with money and an eye to the "future" of the city, with the financial help of other city elite—and the physical labor of convicts—was transforming the insignificant passageway into a "typical" Mexican village. "Each night," Mrs. Sterling wrote in her diary on November 21, 1929, "I pray they will arrest a bricklayer and a plumber." Mrs. Sterling's intention was to provide a tourist attraction and a showcase for the city's multi-ethnic heritage.

The street opened to the public April 20, 1930 with 78 businesses and merchants. "Happiness," wrote Mrs. Sterling, "lingers here as it did in the old days." Avila Adobe on Olvera Street, built in 1818, is believed to be the oldest existing house in Los Angeles.

The size of the Mexican population of Los Angeles has always been underestimated. When Los Angeles became a city in the 1930s there were officially 100,000 Mexicans. In actuality there were probably close to 200,000. In the early days Mestizos (those of mixed heritage) were excluded from the count, and no formal census ever accounted for illegal immigrants. The issue of illegal Mexican immigrants "taking jobs from Americans" is one that dates back to the 1930s when over 13,000 Mexicans in Los Angeles County were deported, presumably to ease Anglo unemployment (which did not improve with the Mexicans gone). Second-generation Mexicans fought such discrimination; these *pachucos* of the 1940s dressed themselves in zoot suits made from great quantities of fabric despite war-time cloth rationing. Since the Japanese in California had been packed off to internment camps, the Chicanos remained to bear the brunt of racial tensions, and rioting broke out in 1943.

After the war, Chicanos began to merge with middle-class White society. Educational opportunities were created by the GI bill and Hispanics began to exercise their political rights against discrimination. In 1949, Ed Roybal was elected to the City Council, the first Chicano since 1881 to hold such a position. He was not, however, able to buy a house in Bella Vista since Mexicans were not allowed to own real estate in this area.

For Los Angeles' Hispanic cultural and religious observances the Mexican community in particular plays a notable public role. Olvera Street, the original Mexican center, has come to represent a sense of place for the Hispanic community in general. Here, on Sundays, up to 13,000 Hispanics attend mass at Our Lady Queen of Angels. And here, Mexican traditions such as *Las Posadas*, the depiction of the journey of Mary and Joseph into Bethlehem, and the Blessing of the Animals, an event dating back to the activities of St. Francis of Assisi in the 13th century, are still celebrated. *Las Posadas* has been celebrated on Olvera Street for more than forty years and family costumes are handed down from generation to generation. For the Blessing of the Animals pets are paraded on Olvera Street on the Saturday before Easter. Iguanas, caged birds, fish, mice, hamsters, snakes, turtles and a plethora of dogs and cats all file around the plaza past the Roman Catholic priest who blesses each animal and sprinkles it with holy water while mariachis provide music.

The two largest Mexican gatherings of the year are the celebration of Independence Day in September and the observance of Cinco de Mayo. Independence Day refers to September 16, 1810, when Father Miguel Hidalgo y Costilla called on his peasant flock in the Mexican town of Dolores to break the chains of Spanish domination. This feat took 11 years to accomplish. The parade celebrating this event has travelled Los Angeles streets annually for over 40 years; the first was comprised of two buses and an ice cream salesman. Today, the parade, which begins at First and Lorena Streets and ends at Belvedere Park, is generally celebrated on the weekend falling before the 16th in an extravaganza which is ballooning in size every year. In 1987 there were more than 300 entries (for comparison, in 1988 there were 114 units in the Rose Parade). The 1987 entries included marching bands, floats, drill teams, horses, TV personalities, politicians, "low-riders," and the *Xipetotec*, feathered dancers from Lincoln Heights dedicated to keeping the Native Mexican past alive. In the evening at Belvedere Park, stage entertainment includes dance troops, mariachi bands and rock groups, and there is a fireworks display. In 1988 more than 100,000 people attended. In West Los Angeles a Mexican cultural arts festival sponsored by the Institute for Cultural Studies celebrates the occasion with folklorico dances, mariachis, salsa bands, Jalisco- and Zacatecas-style music, films, children's activities, exhibits and demonstrations by *artesanos*.

Cinco de Mayo, which is not a major holiday in Mexico, has been built up by Mexican Americans to give the community a sense of identity. Cinco de Mayo commemorates the Mexican battle of 1862 that turned back the invading French army and became a rallying point for Mexico's ultimate liberation; a group of outnumbered Mexican soldiers defeated Napoleon III's army at the city of Puebla. The 1987 Cinco de Mayo celebration in Los Angeles included a parade in Huntington Park with clowns, camels, floats, marching bands, dignitaries, and television and movie stars. The festivities culminated with a party in Lincoln Park. Cinco de Mayo has become an event of such magnitude that every year more than $20 million is spent on corporate advertising and promotion.

The Mexican Day of the Dead celebration at the beginning of November, perpetuated in Los Angeles by incoming Mexicans and the attempts by community leaders to promote ethnic pride, has in recent years caught the attention of the Anglo community. In recent years galleries in Pasadena, Los Angeles and Santa Monica exhibited Day of the Dead art, which is becoming increasingly popular with Anglo collectors. Hispanics in their thirties and forties who never celebrated the day before are now constructing Day of the Dead altars in their homes. Los Angeles' first public Days of the Dead—a traditional Hispanic holiday that honors and remembers the dead—were held under the auspices of Self-Help Graphics (see below), an East Los Angeles community arts organization.

Among the unique artistic treasures of Los Angeles are the East Los Angeles Hispanic murals. Covering the walls of housing developments, alleyways and businesses on major shopping streets these powerful images communicate the struggles and hopes of the people. One of the first, "The Wall that Cracked Open," was painted by Willie Herrón in the early 1970s as a prayer to save his brother, who had been attacked and suffered 100 ice pick wounds.

Chicano art in Los Angeles was fostered by Sister Karen Boccalero, an artist-nun who returned from Rome in 1972 and started "Self-Help Graphics", a workshop with silk-screen equipment. In 1974 Chicano art was exhibited for the first time at a County Museum and in 1990, UCLA's Wight Gallery will inaugurate a major travelling exhibition of Chicano art curated for the first time by Chicanos.

Many traditional Mexican arts are produced in Los Angeles. A 1984 study conducted by Plaza de la Raza documented makers of *piñatas*, paper flowers, ceremonial costumes, saddles, *huaraches* (sandals), *popote* (straw pictures), wrought iron, guitars and harps, silver jewelry, textiles and *migajon* (bread dough sculpture). The items which sell best are those used by the Anglo population, such as jewelry and saddles.

The ultimate tribute to Los Angeles as a Mexican center must be that made by a 19-year-old guitarist who told a Los Angeles *Times* reporter that "there are only two places for a mariachi to become famous, Mexico City and Los Angeles." He spoke from La Boylé, a plaza at Boyle Avenue and First Street where each night for over 30 years mariachis, many of whom live in the area, gather to socialize, join their bands, look for work and hope to "make it" in the great Mexican metropolis of Los Angeles.

■ Cuban

In 1962, when the United States and the Soviet Union seemed to be on the brink of war over the Soviet ballistic missiles in Cuba, terrified Cuban parents put their children on Pan American Flight 95 from Havana to Miami. Some of these children—along with their families (some of whom came via Spain)—found their way to Los Angeles. Many, who had been successful in Cuba, had to get by with menial jobs in the United States.

Today, there are estimated to be about 120,000 Cubans in the Los Angeles Metropolitan area. Most live in Echo Park and Silver Lake with smaller numbers in Culver City, Long Beach, Inglewood, South Gate and Glendale. The majority of this diverse community—businessmen, workers, artists—came in the early 1960s. The established community, through the Cuban Assistance League (an organization created by Abel Perez, the editor of the newspaper *20 de Mayo*, has been helping to settle those who came in the boat lift in 1980 (Marielitos). Paul Revilla, the editor of the second Cuban community newspaper, *La Vox Libre*, is himself a Marielito. There is tension between the old community, who never lived under communism, and the Marielitos, who were raised in Castro's Cuba.

Social clubs in all areas of the city are the primary way the Cubans stay in touch. The big event of the year is the Debutante Ball, held every May at the Hollywood Paladium where about 100 15-year old girls are presented. *Santeria*, an ancient Nigerian religion, is practiced by many Cubans in the area (see pages 119-120, "African").

■ Guatemalan

Los Angeles is the second largest Guatemalan city in the world, with about 100,000 from that country. The majority have come in two waves—a now established community who arrived in the early 1950s and 1960s right after the coup, and the political refugees who arrived in the early 1980s. Like the Salvadorans, many of this later group are asking for political asylum. The Guatemalan community is spread around the city, with concentrations in the Pico-Union area and in Inglewood.

Five to six thousand Maya—Native American inhabitants of Guatemala—live west of downtown Los Angeles. They began to arrive in the city from rural Guatemala during the mid-1970s and increasing numbers have come since 1980 due to the intense military activity in the northwest. Many do not speak Spanish (a reminder that not all of the people in Latin America are Hispanic), and at least one church in the city caters to their needs by holding a service every Saturday in Maya. About 1986 they formed IXIM, "a name taken from the sacred Maya word for corn and an acronym for the Integration of Indigenous Maya." Having their own group as well as a center shelters them to some extent from the strangeness of the city and helps recreate the sense of community that they always had at home. The center also houses a *marimba*, a musical instrument central to ceremonies in the home as well as in church and which has for the Maya an almost sacred nature.

The dynamic textile arts of the Maya are well known to Americans, but the Maya who have come to Los Angeles are not weavers. Textile producers earn a steady living and have enough security in the home country to remain there.

IXIM sponsors two Maya celebrations each year. The Fiesta of Santa Eulalia, a town in northwest Guatemala, is held on the second Saturday in February and includes sporting and cultural events. The former residents of the town of San Miguel holds their celebration on the last Saturday in September. Activities include a dramatization of the town's history, sporting events, music, dance and native foods.

■ Nicaraguan

Since the Sandinista takeover in 1979, Nicaraguans have been resettling in Los Angeles, Miami and Costa Rica. Emigration increased in the mid-1980s as teenagers started to leave Nicaragua before they were drafted. As wages continue to be slashed and jobs eliminated, the middle class and skilled professionals have begun to leave in large numbers. Today's Nicaraguan emigrant is often not a political refugee but rather someone who simply wishes to hold a job. Private companies bus the emigrants to Guatemala, where they pay up to $1,500 to smugglers to guide them on an illegal trek across Mexico and into Texas, where they can catch a bus to Los Angeles or Miami.

There are probably more than 50,000 Nicaraguans in Southern California, with the community divided along Sandinista/Contra lines. Increasingly these newcomers are professional people. Gilberto Cuadra, president of the Superior Council of Private Enterprise, told the Los Angeles *Times* that more Nicaraguan architects and engineers now live in Los Angeles than in Managua. As more Nicaraguans resettle here and send money home, more emigrants are expected to be able to finance their own escape.

Salvadoran

Los Angeles is now the second largest Salvadoran city in the world with more than 350,000 Salvadorans in the county—refugees from the brutal civil war and poverty. They are concentrated, with other Central Americans, in the Pico-Union area, Hollywood, Huntington Park and the San Fernando Valley.

Since the early 1980s El Salvador has been the bloodiest country in the hemisphere; tens of thousands of civilians have been killed. Smugglers charge more than $1,000 per person to bring individuals from El Salvador to Tijuana by plane followed by a risky trip across the border and a truck ride to a Hispanic neighborhood in Los Angeles. Some are also brought in by American sanctuary groups.

The Reagan administration, however, labelled these people "economic migrants" and sent about 50,000 back. Those—about half—who arrived here after January 1, 1982, do not qualify for general amnesty. According to Susan Candel of the legal department at El Rescate, the largest organization in the city helping Central American refugees, the number of refugees asking for political asylum has gone up 1,300 percent. As only one to three percent of these requests are granted, those helping the Salvadorans usually feel that it is better for them not to request asylum.

South American

No South American people live in Los Angeles in large numbers, but there are concentrations of Peruvians, Chileans, Argentinians and Brazilians. The 50,000 to 60,000 Peruvians live primarily in Southgate, Huntington Park, North Hollywood and the San Fernando Valley. Almost all came to the United States looking to escape the bleak economic conditions of their country.

About 45,000 Argentinians live in Southern California. Most have left Argentina because of the economic conditions and were attracted to Southern California by the climate and the success stories of previous Argentine immigrants. Professional people and businessmen immigrated during the 1960s, followed by blue-collar workers and small businessmen between 1976 and 1982. The Argentine residents of Southern California are a diverse group and live in many parts of the city; they tend not to identify with the Hispanic communities from Mexico and Central America. The majority maintain no direct links with Argentina, although many, because of lower costs, send their children "home" to be educated. The community sporadically publishes newspapers and sponsors radio programs, but most of these ventures are short-lived.

The Chileans in the Los Angeles area—about 16,000—began to arrive after the 1973 coup. Some may return now that that regime has ended. The largest Chilean community in California is in San José, and a San Francisco telephone line is continuously updated with news about the home country. The Los Angeles Chilean consulate puts out a newsletter twice a month and hosts a September 18 celebration of Chilean Independence Day. A restaurant/delicatessan on Melrose, the Rincón Chileno, serves as a hub for the community.

The Brazilians (about 10,000) have immigrated with their musical groups. Embrasamba and Viva Brasil are two which provide nonstop samba music. Even with their small numbers the Brazilians maintain radio shows, nightclubs and restaurants, the latter featuring Feo Joiada, the national dish of Brazil—black beans, pork and manioc flour.

Blessing of the Animals, Olvera Street

Chinatown

Asian

More than twenty Asian/Pacific cultures are represented in Southern California. Chinese, Japanese, Indians, Filipinos, Koreans, Vietnamese, Cambodians, Laotians, Thais, Samoans, Tongans, Hawaiians and Guamanians comprise the bulk of the Los Angeles County Asian community. There are also small groups from Bangladesh, Burma, Indonesia, Malaysia, Nepal, Pakistan, Singapore and Sri Lanka.

The Chinese, who began to arrive in the middle of the nineteenth century, were one of the earliest ethnic groups in Los Angeles. The Japanese came after the Chinese and to a large extent replaced them as a labor force after the Chinese Exclusion Act of 1882. Indians first came in the 1960s. All others began arriving in substantial numbers in the mid-1970s—the largest concentration of Southeast Asian refugees in the nation are now here—and Asians are now the fastest-growing group in the County after Hispanics (by the year 2000, if the current trend continues, they will be the fastest-growing group). Since 1980 the percentage of Asian/Pacific Islanders has risen from about six percent of the population to almost twelve percent. Between 1970 and 1980 the Asian Pacific population of Los Angeles County grew 92 percent, from 238,000 to 457,000. It has doubled again since 1980, with about one million Asians and Pacific Islanders living in Los Angeles County in 1988. Another major increase to about two million is expected by the year 2000 (from 11.8 percent to 17.3 percent of the county population). Asian/Pacific Islanders now comprise a third of all legal immigrants coming into Los Angeles County.

Los Angeles has the largest Korean population outside of Seoul, the largest Filipino population outside Manila, the largest Japanese population outside Japan and the largest Asian population in the United States. Individually and collectively these groups are making their mark on the city. These peoples now provide more than 500 sushi bars and more than 300 Thai and 600 Korean restaurants. There are in addition about 200 hostess clubs—Asian establishments that provide drinks and female companionship for Asian businessmen—around the County, the largest number located in Koreatown (see page 88) but with some also in Torrance, the San Gabriel Valley and other locations. Asian games such as "Go" are being pursued by Anglos as well as Asians at increasing numbers of clubs. UCLA's freshman class in 1987 was 25 percent Asian American and the foreign student body in 1988 was 44 percent Asian. Increased interest in the Pacific Rim has led UCLA to double the number of its faculty in Japanese and Chinese studies, including three at the law school. The strong social, cultural and economic presence of these peoples prompted the Los Angeles *Herald Examiner* in May 1988 to undertake a 21-part series examining Los Angeles' Asian Community. But not all organizations have caught up with the increasing Asian population. One *Herald Examiner* reporter noted that there are only 108 Asian officers out of more than 7,000 in the Los Angeles Police Department. In fact, the Asian community cites the lack of Asian officers as a reason for the large number of racially motivated crimes directed against Asians. The Los Angeles Police Department has responded that the problem is not lack in qualifications but lack in ability to speak English and is now allowing applicants to receive tutoring and speech lessons.

It must never be assumed, however, that there is a single unified Asian community. Each of these peoples have a unique language, culture, sense of purpose and reason for leaving their home country. Koreans tend to be entrepreneurs and are likely to enter the United States with money; Thais come for economic gain; Vietnamese and Cambodians immigrate to escape conditions in their home countries. These groups tend to concentrate and most have their own television and radio programs and their own newspapers. Nine new Asian dailies and dozens of weeklies and bimonthlies started publication between 1980 and 1987. There is one Vietnamese daily and four weeklies. The four weekly Filipino papers are all published in English with a combined circulation of 120,000. One of these Filipino papers, the *California Examiner*, gets half of its advertising from non-Filipino businesses (as do many other Asian papers), averages 50 pages a week and has correspondents in Washington, New York, San Francisco and Manila. In the fall of 1988 radio station KAZN became the first in North America to have 100 percent Asian programming, with four- to six-hour blocks devoted to Japanese-, Chinese-, Korean-, Filipino- and Vietnamese-language programming. On television, Channel 18 is increasingly becoming the voice of the Los Angeles-area Asian community.

In Los Angeles, as well as across the country, Asians are seen as the "hot new ethnic market." Since their median family income is higher than the norm, the number of advertisements directed at them on television, radio and through magazines is increasing. They are potential consumers for items ranging from life insurance to trendy clothes. Koreans, Chinese from Hong Kong and Taiwan, and particularly the Japanese have become active participants in the housing market. Even though studies show that many Asians bring from their home countries a scepticism of politics, their increasing numbers and traditional voter apathy have attracted the attention of politicians. At the same time it is clear that they are far from a unified political group; a solid bloc of Asian voters does not exist for either major political party.

Asian Americans, in general, have done well in Los Angeles. First-generation immigrants have succeeded as small business owners and as skilled technicians. One of the most important factors in the business success of Asians is the underground banking system called *hui* in Chinese, *kye* in Korean and *tanomoshi* in Japanese. In a typical encounter within this system about a dozen friends meet once a month and each person contributes the same amount to a pot that can reach hundreds of thousands of dollars. These clubs are not illegal here, although they do operate outside of United States banking laws and can offer extraordinarily high rates of interest to those willing to put up cash. Every month a different member of the group gets the whole amount. The system is based on trust and only requires that the group meet enough times so that each person gets the pot at least once.

Later generations of Asians have excelled as students. In 1987 55 percent of Asian-American high-school students were eligible for admission to the University of California, compared with the county average of 28.6 percent; nearly half get college degrees. Asian parents often take an active role in expanding their children's learning opportunities. This emphasis on education (a Japanese San Pedro fisherman is reputed to have told his son that if he graduated from college, "I will proudly meet our ancestors in heaven") is particularly true of the Asians who arrived before 1965, who tend to be from the middle and upper classes and who have a work ethic which corresponds well to the American. Later arrivals, particularly the refugees who have little education and low incomes, have had a more difficult time adjusting. Refugee children are often homeless and turn to crime, drugs and gangs through their alienation. "For many of these children," writes a reporter for the Los Angeles *Times*, America is not so much a new start as it is a continuation of their rootlessness." It is sobering to contrast these refugee children with the middle class and acculturated Japanese-American teenagers who quickly learn American rites including that of Prom Night.

A United Way Report in 1986 noted that poverty among Asians had risen from 9 to 13 percent in the last decade and a following report notes that with the burgeoning Asian population "there is evidence of terrible and untold human need." There is another side, this report tells us, to the stereotype that Asians are the "model minority"; in Los Angeles today there are not only orphaned children but battered women, single parents, elderly and adolescents who are in desperate need of help. Mental health services are badly needed for war-torn refugees, and money for all these services is in short supply. Added strife arises, for example, when newly-arrived merchants of both new and established groups underprice goods in order to survive and are perceived as a threat by those more acculturated.

Ironically, opposed to the common belief that Asians always take care of the elderly, the 1988 report found this group to be the neediest and the least provided for of all Asians in the city. While Chinese communities for Asian senior citizens are functioning, apparently well, in both Chinatown and Monterey Park, Asian seniors are having to learn to adapt to the pros and cons of living away from their families; some note that there are advantages to the independence but that this is often not enough to offset the loneliness. But the elderly, too, learn American ways; in September of 1988 Chinatown senior citizens organized a protest march against their housing project. Increasingly Asian/Pacific peoples are feeling the squeeze between the needs of children and the needs of parents. As they become more Americanized, the extended family contines to dissolve.

Westernization is affecting Los Angeles' Asian community in other ways. Women may be most vulnerable in the conflict. Young girls, particularly from the recent Vietnamese, Cambodian and Laotian refugee immigrations, are caught between the traditional needs of the family and the modern emphasis on independence, between a culture which treats women as subservient and a culture which increasingly encourages female initiative. Women are faced with the complexities of intermarriage, constantly increasing, primarily between White men and Asian women (Korean women reputedly "outmarry" more than any other group). Asian women too, in ever greater numbers are entering the work force, shaking in additional ways the traditional Asian beliefs in the primacy of the family. Some of these women have achieved positions of some power; Mayumi Shirai is president and CEO of ASAHI Homecast Corporation, a Japanese television network (airing in Los Angeles on Channel 18) which is the biggest of its kind in the United States; and Betty Ton-Chu, a Chinese American, is one of the founders and CEO of Trust Savings Bank.

About 180,000 Asians live in the San Gabriel Valley; most are in the western cities, particularly Monterey Park and Alhambra, but with increasing house prices more are settling in the eastern sector of the Valley. One plaza in the city of San Gabriel has a Filipino grocery, a Vietnamese cafe, a Japanese bakery, an Indonesian delicatessen and Taiwanese, Chinese and Japanese restaurants. It is not surprising, therefore, that every aspect of these increasingly Asian communities has been subject to rearrangement. Schools, for example, send notes home in Cantonese, Mandarin and Vietnamese as well as English. White Americans find that they must accommodate alternate ways of seeing the world; Dave Carmany, an Alhambra city planner, notes that a street closure could not be enacted "when a Chinese restaurant owner became livid . . . the owner said access wasn't the problem. He said the location of his front door, the cash register and the main dining room were all decided by the compass of the *fungshui* (a diviner of heavenly spirits). He said closing off the one street would be analogous to cutting off one of the heads of the five-headed dragon."

One result of the growing number of Asians in Los Angeles is the presence of the College of Buddhist Studies on South New Hampshire Avenue. The College was instituted in 1983 by the Buddhist Sangha Council of Southern California in answer to the growing desire for more Buddhist education than the temples could provide. The College offers a Bachelor of Arts and a Master of Arts in Buddhist Studies. The brochure notes that the "College offers students of Buddhism a unique opportunity to experience a comprehensive in-depth study of Buddhism from a non-sectarian point of view, while also promoting knowledge and understanding of the different schools and cultural traditions within Buddhism. Courses are taught by scholars and masters of a variety of traditions, taking advantage of Southern California's uniqueness: the only place in the world where all Buddhist ethnic practice and denominations are found, allowing the student the chance to study not only the philosophy and psychology of Buddhism, but also to experience its richness of practice."

■ Chinese

The 1850 census for the Pueblo of Los Angeles records two Chinese—
Ah Luce and Ah Fou, both male house servants—among its 1,610
residents. One of the earliest ethnic groups in the city, the Chinese
were the first to be brought to California as a labor force. Cantonese
were the first to arrive, escaping overpopulation and civil war in Southeast China. Men could obtain passage by a "credit-ticket," whereby a
merchant in Canton and a San Francisco representative paid his fare
which he eventually had to repay. Some Chinese were attracted by the
Gold Rush; others, starting in 1865, were brought in large numbers to
work on the Southern Pacific Railroad. By 1870 the former railroad
workers had pushed the Chinese population of the city from 234 to
4,000. Over a thousand others worked on the San Fernando Tunnel,
dug between 1874 and 1876, with many losing their lives in the process.

By the 1870s, the Chinese were the largest foreign group in California,
making up one tenth of the population and one fourth of the wage labor
force. The vast majority were men, since they came as laborers. By
1890 there were 106,500 Chinese in the United States but less than
4,000 were female.

Throughout the nineteenth century the Chinese worker was seen as a
threat to jobs and democracy and came to be resented by the White
population. In those days the supply of Chinese workers who could
obey but not bargain appeared limitless. Antagonism against the Chinese surpassed anti-Native American and anti-Mexican sentiment, and
riots with the Chinese as targets became common. A violent outbreak
took place in 1871, the most severe racial conflict in the city until the
Watts riots almost a century later. David L. Clark describes the conflict
as follows:

> . . . . a mob surged through Chinatown shooting, stabbing,
> lynching, and looting. At least 19 Chinese were left dead. A
> number of citizens rescued Chinese people from the mob in-
> cluding Robert W. Widney, one of the founders of the Univer-
> sity of Southern California. Armed with a large Colt revolver, he
> held attackers and escorted many Chinese to safety. Judge
> Wilson Hugh Gray hid Chinese in the cellar of his house at
> Broadway and Seventh. For years afterward, on the Chinese
> New Year, he found anonymous presents at his door.

Anti-Chinese cartoons appeared in newspapers in the late 1870s and
1880s, reflecting the fears that White workers would be neglected in

favor of Chinese. In 1880 P.W. Dooner in the *Last Days of the Republic* issued a warning to the people of the twentieth century that the Chinese were intent on taking over the world. This warning, in a full-length book, was a fictionalized but (to Dooner) obvious account of what lay ahead. As described in an ancient Chinese plan the scenario was as follows:

> The traditions and the policy of China teach and require that she shall aim to rule the whole world; and she has been awaiting the march of events to initiate, by appropriate signs, the era of her conquests. If there are those who doubt that such is indeed the conviction of the Chinese people, and hence the policy of the Empire, all such are referred to the international correspondence between that government and our own. This singular hallucination breathes thoughout almost every state paper issued under the authority of the Emperor.

In fact, the Chinese in Los Angeles seemed far from scheming. Most were engaged in vegetable farming and peddling—Chinese immigrants organized one of the earliest produce markets in the city at Ninth and San Pedro—or in performing most of the early Southern California agricultural labor. The latter made possible the rapid expansion of the citrus industry. Those not working in agriculture took low-paying jobs as domestics, or in restaurants, laundries or curio shops. In 1900 more than 25,000 Chinese listed their occupation as "laundryman," and by 1920, out of a labor force of about 46,000, more than 12,000 were working in Chinese laundries and over 11,000 in Chinese restaurants. It was their industriousness and growing numbers that bred contempt; hostility from the Anglo community persuaded the Chinese, initially, not to set up competitive businesses.

The new immigrants lived in a ghetto. Los Angeles' Chinatown is over 100 years old and was originally located east of Olvera Street Plaza. It began in a section of the city known as "Calle de los Negroes" or "Nigger Alley" and housed the most unfortunate in the city. "Nigger Alley" became Chinatown in the 1880s, and by 1890 more than 50 percent of the city's approximately 2,000 Chinese lived in the vicinity. Described as a dimly lit community with narrow streets and alleys, it must have seemed distant from the Los Angeles of the promoters. The Anglos came to Chinatown for two reasons—to eat chop suey and other Americanized Chinese dishes or to engage in some illicit activity, such as prostitution, drug use or gambling. It is estimated that there were 100 opium dens in the area around the turn of the century. When the drug was outlawed in 1912, the price shot up and, presumably, most of the dens were closed.

Demolition of this original Chinatown began in 1933 to make way for the new railroad terminal. New Chinatown, which opened in 1938, was moved a few blocks north and east, and for the first time the Chinese owned the land themselves—bought for 75 cents a square foot. In the new location the emphasis was on providing a modern, comfortable shopping area. When it opened, New Chinatown had 18 stores and a beancake factory. It was this relocation 50 years ago that provided the original impetus for the dispersion of the Chinese community.

At the same time that New Chinatown was being organized, society leader Christine Sterling, who had been responsible for the redevelopment of Olvera Street, proposed China City. This block-long development had its roots in Hollywood rather than China. Although one Chinese resident of the time described it as having the "atmosphere of a small Chinese village," a set designer from Paramount had collaborated in the conception, and Cecil B. de Mille donated studio props and "Chinese" costumes. Later, scenes from "The Good Earth" would be shot there. In June 1938 China City opened at Ord and Spring. There were serpentine streets, twisting alleys and vendors selling food from carts and rickshaws. The entrance was through an ornate gate, and from the main street, Dragon Road, the Road of the Lotus ran to the Court of Four Seasons. The town hall was in the shape of a pirate junk. Happily, perhaps, for the Chinese of Los Angeles, China City was destroyed by fire six months after it opened. New Chinatown, on the other hand, was developed by Peter Soo Hoo for the Chinese, as opposed to the tourists, and for generations of Angelenos it is the only Chinatown they have ever known. It is not surprising, however, that after more than 50 years the area has seen major changes. When it was built, Chinatown was a homogeneous community whose residents all came from Canton and spoke the same dialect. Today there are a great diversity of Chinese (speaking Cantonese, Mandarin, Szechwan and other dialects)—including a group from Vietnam and other Asians and some Hispanics. Many Chinese-American political and cultural leaders live in other parts of the city and speak English rather than Chinese.

The Chinese exclusion acts of 1882 and 1892, each of which barred Chinese immigration for ten years, were the direct result of the nineteenth-century "yellow menace mania." The Geary Act in Los Angeles allowed the Chinese to be driven forcibly from Norwalk, Burbank, Vernon, Pasadena and what is today Hollywood. In 1902 the federal exclusion act was made permanent and not repealed until 1943. The Chinese population was reduced by almost half from 1890 to 1920. New laws permitted only limited immigration between 1943 and 1965. It was, therefore, not until after 1965 that the Chinese population in Los

Angeles began to mushroom; between 1960 and 1970, it increased 84 percent. In December 1988 1,300 Chinese took the oath of citizenship from District Judge Ronald Lew, one of three Chinese-American federal judges. Unlike San Francisco and New York, the great majority, about 90 percent, of Los Angeles County's Chinese population resides outside of Chinatown.

Today it is difficult to comprehend the early attitudes toward the Chinese. The approximately 170,000 people of Chinese descent in Los Angeles County are an integral, active and positive component of the city. But the early reaction to the Chinese, while extreme, is not an atypical one. Immigrant groups who arrive in any city with little money and few resources but with the will and energy to survive are often the targets of discrimination and ridicule. As these peoples become acculturated and familiar, however, the attitudes of the native population become increasingly tolerant.

The Chinese community in Los Angeles today is composed of many different groups who have been here for varying lengths of time. There are linguistic differences, the most obvious between Cantonese and Mandarin; varying kinship relations, from bloodline to clan associations; political differences, Communist and anti-Communist; numerous geographical origins, such as Hong Kong, the Republic of China and Singapore; and divergent cultural preferences ranging from traditional to assimilationist. These diverse attitudes can and have produced tensions within the Chinese communities.

The Chinese population is generally well educated and many of the new professionals have moved to the suburbs. Businessmen from Taiwan and Hong Kong have invested in Chinatown property, making it among the most expensive real estate in the city. A $30-50 million proposed development on Hill Street, financed by an Indonesian-Chinese banking institution will include (if the project, now in doubt, is realized) a long-desired Chinese cultural center including a theater, community rooms, classrooms, an exhibit hall, and the headquarters for the bank and other commercial and retail buildings. Chinese investors from overseas have also purchased about one third of the land in Monterey Park in the San Gabriel Valley. Known as the "Chinese Beverly Hills," it is the largest Chinese suburban community in the United States. But for the many Chinese who move to the suburbs and take on the American "good life," there are others who enter the city, live in tenements near Chinatown and are exploited for their labor. The complicated and often exotic history of the Chinese in Los Angeles has not ended.

In the 1980s many more Chinese continued to reside outside of China-town than in it. Economic mobility has led to territorial mobility and different ways of defining "home." The residents of Monterey Park, unlike those in Chinatown, consider their property to be private rather than community-shared, an attitude which leads to ethnic conflict. The transformation of Monterey Park into an Asian community was the direct doing of Frederic Hsieh, a young Chinese-American developer who in the 1970s began to buy up the property for the next Chinatown. It was an ideal choice: Monterey Park is in a mixed neighborhood which White residents have been vacating, only eight miles from Chinatown and near freeways. Hsieh's vision has indeed been realized. In 1970 Monterey Park was 14 percent Asian, and by 1988 it was over 50 percent (60 percent of whom are Chinese)—the highest concentra-tion of any city in the country.

Monterey Park has been described as having the feel of an international boom town. A dozen Chinese-run banks with combined deposits of more than $400 million have opened since 1979. Four Chinese-language newspapers with world-wide circulation are published here. Altogether there are five daily papers, three of them with a Southern California circulation approaching 50,000. The *International Daily News* averages 56 pages a day, uses full color and has full-time news bureaus in San Francisco, Vancouver, Toronto, New York, Texas, Taipei and Hong Kong, and a correspondent in Washington. The *World Daily News* even has Nancy Lin, "the closest thing in Southern California to a Chinese Ann Landers." Lin writes "Friends Mailbox," an advice column that is sponsored by the Asian Pacific Family Center in Rosemead and attends to the problems of the Chinese immigrant community. There are topics familiar to Americans, such as parent-child relationships, but Lin draws on Chinese culture when dealing with topics such as extramarital affairs ("affairs are a cancer to family happiness") and common sense when trying to offset the loneliness and bewilderment of the immigrant ("get your driver's license"). Lin thinks Ann Landers and Dear Abby are "great . . . but I don't think I get many ideas from them. It's a different culture." Monterey Park also boasts sixty Chinese restaurants and several Chinese-run nightclubs.

Unfortunately, the ever-growing Asian population and the conversion from town to city has upset some of the longtime residents—Anglo, Latino and Asian. The newcomers, they claim, do not integrate well, they drive erratically, push into lines and mainly do not learn English (Monterey Park has been called the place where Chinese live who cannot speak English). Some of the older residents have felt alienated enough to move both homes and businesses to other areas of the city.

In Hacienda Heights, in the east San Gabriel Valley, there sits on a ridge "a constellation of pagoda-style buildings with glazed-tile roofs, broad eaves and random highlights of green and gold." The Hsi Lai Temple is the largest Buddhist monastery and temple complex in the Western Hemisphere; a fourteen-acre, ten-building, $25 million complex housing 40 Buddhist monks and nuns which opened in November 1988 as the national headquarters of Fo Kuang Shan, Taiwan's prominent Buddhist organization. The opening of the monastery was accompanied by the first meeting of the World Fellowship of Buddhists held outside of Asia; two Americans were elected as vice-presidents emphasizing the Temple's commitment to a united Buddhism in America. The main shrine boasts a gold-plated, two-ton chandelier brought from Japan, 10,000 statues of the Buddha, and can accommodate 700 worshippers. The Reverend Shih Yung Kai states the purpose of the temple as carrying out "an educational and cultural program concerning Buddhism and Chinese culture. We will have Sunday services in the main shrine. We will also organize seminars, for example, on Chinese calligraphy." The complex also includes a library, meditation hall and memorial pagoda. At the same time as this elaborate monastery opened its doors, Chinese herbalists quietly continued to practice ancient remedies from small shops in Chinatown where doctors dispense cures ranging from acupuncture to rattlesnake-steeped whiskey.

Chinese New Year is one of the most well-known celebrations in the city; in 1989 tens of thousands turned out to watch the parade. For a week in February, firecrackers, parades, thundering gongs and floats pervade Chinatown. In 1988, a 120-foot "five-clawed, almost-iridescent dragon" wove "its way through the streets, supported by 22 martial arts aficionados." Other attractions included smaller dragons, exhibits of martial arts and traditional forms of entertainment. At the 1988 festivities, perhaps in acknowledgment of Los Angeles' ethnic diversity, there were also Scottish bagpipes and Mexican drummers.

◾ Japanese

Los Angeles County, with about 200,000 Japanese, has the largest community outside of Japan. (The Japanese Consulate estimates nearly 300,000 in the Los Angeles area.) The Japanese began coming to Los Angeles later than the Chinese; many started by working as migrant laborers on large farms throughout the state but gradually moved to Los Angeles to start their own businesses. One estimate puts the 1896 Japanese population at around 100 (there were about 1,000 in Los

Angeles County), with at least 16 Japanese-owned restaurants. The Yokohama restaurant, in business around the turn of the century, had four waiters, two cooks and a dishwasher. Unlike most European immigrants in the late nineteenth and early twentieth centuries, these Issei (first generation) were relatively well educated.

The population increased for a number of reasons. Between 2,000 and 3,000 came from San Francisco after the 1906 earthquake and others moved to Los Angeles to escape the anti-Japanese movement which at the time was more extreme in northern California. Japanese clothes designer Riye Yoshizawa, now in her eighties, recalls that in 1910 her father grew flowers where the Los Angeles Hilton now stands. By 1910 there were more Japanese in Los Angeles than any city in the United States except San Francisco, and by 1920 nearly half of Los Angeles' non-White population was Japanese.

They so thoroughly took over the farming industry that during the 1920s and 1930s, 90 percent of the produce consumed in Los Angeles was raised by Japanese. From growing they moved to wholesaling and retailing. Through dealing with other Japanese in the food industry and by making funds available for incoming Japanese or those who wanted to expand their businesses, they developed a self-sufficient limited ethnic economy.

The Japanese were among the pioneers of the fishing industry on the West Coast and by 1929 had helped make San Pedro the nation's number one fishing port. Their isolated fishing village of about 1000 people on Terminal Island, complete with Shinto Temple, resembled those in Japan. In Little Tokyo, by 1915, the Japanese owned more than three quarters of the small businesses. This group also worked as gardeners and were responsible for much of the landscaping in today's Los Angeles. By 1940, when Los Angeles County with almost 37,000 Japanese had become the undisputed population center of Japanese-America, a large group of Japanese were living in the Sawtelle Boulevard area—in those days far out in the western suburbs. This group was comprised almost exclusively of gardeners and many of the Japanese nurseries have remained.

Much of the history of the Japanese in Los Angeles concerns their ostracism by the White community and the resultant isolation. Like the Chinese, they were resented for their industriousness, and Whites saw these new entrepreneurs as a threat. As a result the Japanese had no choice but to continue patronizing their own and therefore the mainlanders were almost as isolated as the Japanese Americans on Terminal

Island. When the Japanese attacked Pearl Harbor, the isolated Los Angeles Japanese were easy targets of White resentment and were immediately accused of spying and sabotage. The charges were ludicrous. They were said to have conveyed to the Japanese government items such as charts of the coastal waters which were readily available to anyone for 25 cents. Nevertheless, on February 19, 1942, Executive Order 9066 was signed, authorizing the War Department to carry out the evacuation of all the Japanese on the West Coast. Thousands, two thirds of whom were native-born American citizens, began moving to the relocation camps inland, east of the Sierra Nevada mountains, where they would spend the war. Most lost all of their savings and possessions in this process. It is estimated that $300 to $400 million in capital was lost.

After the war the fishermen of Terminal Island were not allowed to return to their village and many former executives had to take jobs as gardeners, but with time new opportunities did arise. Most of the returning Japanese Americans resettled in areas of the city other than Little Tokyo. As a result Little Tokyo became, for some time, a daytime community. The Nisei (second generation) entered professions and their children entered the mainstream of Los Angeles society.

In addition to the 190,000 Japanese Americans living in Los Angeles County (almost 30 percent of all the Japanese in North America), nearly 200,000 Los Angeles area residents carry Japanese passports. The total Japanese concentration has been increasing at a rate of 15 percent annually since 1980. There are three daily Japanese newspapers in the city; the largest, *Rafu Shimpo*, has a circulation of about 22,000.

With time and acculturation the Japanese language and religions are, to a large extent, being replaced by American culture, and the older generation fears the complete loss of ethnic identity. A United Way study indicates that of all Asian/Pacific peoples in Los Angeles the Japanese have the lowest percentage (one percent) maintaining extended families, one indication that they are likely the most Westernized group. In a show of their learned American-style activism in 1970, the Japanese-American community successfully protested the widening of Sawtelle Boulevard in West Los Angeles, thereby saving the distinct Japanese character of the street.

Trying to preserve Japanese culture is the Japanese Cultural Institute in Gardena (a Japanese-American organization has been at or near the site of the present institute since the 1920s) which aims to "perpetuate the culture and retain it into the third and fourth generation," according to

Paul Tsukahara, a Gardena Councilman. The institute is a focal point for many activities in the Japanese community and attracts Japanese-American senior citizens, Nisei, Sansei (third generation) and Yonsei (fourth generation). Classes are offerred in bonsai, *ikebana* (flower arranging), Japanese language, martial arts, ballroom dancing, English, folk and Japanese dancing and a form of Japanese folk singing called *karaoke*.

Little Tokyo, the area around First and San Pedro Streets, was so named in 1908. The oldest Japanese settlement on the North American mainland, it was founded in 1885 when an ex-seaman named Kame opened a restaurant on the west side of Los Angeles Street. Today the Buddhist Temple, the Higashi Honganji at 505 E. 3rd St, remains active, administered by the Reverend Noriaki Ito who was born in Japan and brought to the United States when he was six. Little Tokyo has expanded from its modest beginnings, today sporting modern plazas and elegant department stores catering to an elite Japanese taste. Ambitious plans for a large municipal building, a 430-room hotel with traditional Japanese rooms and suites with futons and tatami mats, stores, hundreds of apartments, a plaza, and a museum to be based in the Buddhist Temple are being considered for the near future. The New Otani Hotel and Garden is a focal point for many Japanese cultural activities; chefs demonstrate cooking techniques and there are tea ceremonies and classes in flower arranging, calligraphy and the art of wearing a kimono. Japanese merchandise can be obtained at Matsuzakaya, a branch of one of Japan's oldest department stores. The Japanese-American Cultural and Community Center caters to ethnic arts and cultural events.

The Japanese presence in the Los Angeles area is strong. There are ever-increasing numbers of sushi bars and as of August 1988, 563 Japanese restaurants. Los Angeles has become the noodle- (*ramen*) making capital of the United States, with at least six companies in the area. More and more boutiques carry Japanese-designed clothes for both men and women. One store in Little Tokyo, "Tokyo Bridal and Tuxedo," is the only place that rents American wedding outfits to Japanese tourists who, since Japanese movie star Yuzo Kayama was married in Hollywood more than ten years ago, have been coming to Los Angeles in increasing numbers for their nuptials. At about $5,000 for a six-day wedding trip, the cost is about one quarter the price of being married in Japan.

A Japanese architect, Arata Isozaki, designed the new Museum of Contemporary Art, and Japanese-designed homes have influenced Los Angeles architecture. Art galleries in the city are replete with shows by Japanese and Japanese-American artists, and the Museum of Contemporary Art in 1986 hosted a major exhibit titled "Tokyo: Form and Spirit." The Los Angeles County Museum of Art, which houses a large Japanese collection, opened its 32,000-square-foot Pavilion for Japanese Art in September 1988; "a sublime setting for the sublime art" according to critic Sam Hall Kaplan. Los Angeles' key role in Japan's foreign trade prompted Japan's Ministry of Foreign Affairs in conjunction with the Japanese consulate and local business art groups to sponsor in October 1988 an 18-day Japan "Week." The festival featured a diverse sampling of Japanese society, including Bunraku, films, an invitational golf tournament and a discussion of trade issues.

The integrity of the city's Japanese community was perhaps best described by the wife of a Japanese businessman who was temporarily residing in Los Angeles. After a visit to the East Coast, she noted that returning to California is "like coming back to Japan. You can get Japanese food, Japanese TV and you can live without using English." The Japanese now own so much downtown office space that a circulating joke names Los Angeles as Japan's fastest-growing city.

While Japanese furnishings, clothing and food pervade the city, Little Tokyo continues to be the traditional center for ceremonies and social and cultural gatherings. The most extensive festival is Nisei Week, held each August. It was conceived during the Depression as a way of boosting business for Little Tokyo merchants as well as a way of unifying Japanese Americans and the tradition-oriented community. Harkening back to the summer festival of Japan it is nonetheless a distinctly Japanese-American event, opened by a Shinto priest offering prayers in both Japanese and English. The parades have included floats, hundreds of kimono-clad *ondo* folk dancers, marching bands and dignitaries. For a week the area teems with cultural events, tea ceremonies, exhibits on bonsai, *ikebana*, sports events such as karate tournaments, along with foot and bicycle races, carnivals, food and constant music. Fine arts performances include both Japanese-American and traditional Japanese offerings. In 1986 about 50,000 people attended the festivities, about half of whom were non-Japanese. Companies based in Japan take advantage of the gathering by sending public relations representatives to tell of forthcoming branch offices in Los Angeles.

ASIAN

Oshogatsu, the Japanese New Year, is celebrated on January 1st at the Japanese American Cultural and Community Center, where the celebration opens with archers launching arrows to ward off evil spirits for the coming year. Traditional dancing, music and food follows. Other Little Tokyo-based events include the appearance of a true Japanese-American product called "Shogun Santa" who has become a Christmas tradition. A mix of Kris Kringle and a Samurai warrior, "Shogun Santa" has the children sit in his lap and relay their wishes. Children's Day—combining Girls' Day (March 3) and Boys' Day (May 5) is celebrated for two days. Taiko drummers, martial arts demonstrations, arts and crafts workshops, puppet shows, films, storytellers of Japanese folk tales, Japanese dance troupes, children's choirs, origami demonstrations, magic shows, games, races and radio-controlled aircraft and cars are all organized for Japanese youngsters.

Outside of Little Tokyo, the 1,450-year-old Oban Festival is held at various Buddhist Temples. The festival, originally a strictly religious observance to mark and honor the return of the souls of the dead, has become in Los Angeles a mixture of Japanese and American religion and entertainment. There are games, cultural displays and food, including such non-Japanese fare as nachos, tamales and hot dogs. But the most important aspect remains the traditional dancing which reenacts the first Oban dance of A.D. 538 by the disciples of the Buddha, to celebrate the release from hell and entry into nirvana of the mother of one of the disciples. In Los Angeles the religious observances are often held far in advance of the festivals, which are intended primarily as fundraisers for the church. The major temples in Southern California, therefore, schedule their festivities on different days so that church members have a chance to go to other's festivals. For more than 25 years an annual Japanese cultural show in Gardena (in September) has featured Japanese arts, including a landscaped garden with pond and *koi*.

The economic presence of the Japanese in Los Angeles is so strong that the Japanese community has noted on several occasions that this has become an issue of concern to some in the Anglo population; the city offers a base to an estimated 900 Japanese businesses. The Japanese community is also one of the few groups in the city with strong economic ties to its home country on an on-going basis. In 1988 Japanese real estate purchases in Los Angeles totalled more than $3 billion, or 18 percent of Japanese purchases in the country. The Japanese and other Asians who have a passion for both California real estate and golf have bought at least ten of the more than 300 golf courses in the Los Angeles area. Lest we think that the Japanese have finally been received without prejudice, the 1988 Japanese purchase of the exclusive Riviera Country Club is a revealing case. Some members felt that it was "almost un-American selling it to the Japanese" and many said they have "visions of sushi bars near the sand traps."

■ Cambodian

In 1980 the Census indicated only about 16,000 Cambodians in all of the United States. Today about 50,000 (estimates for Southern California range from 30,000 to over 80,000) refugees from the war-torn country have settled in the Los Angeles area, primarily in Long Beach (the largest Cambodian group in the country) and the surrounding communities.

The Khemara Buddikaram, the area's oldest and largest Cambodian Buddhist Temple, began in a yellow three-bedroom suburban house in a quiet residential corner of Lakewood. In August 1987, Southern California Cambodians realized a ten-year-old-dream when the temple re-opened in Long Beach as one component of the largest religious, cultural and social Cambodian center in the country. Patterned after the pagodas of Cambodia, the new Khemara Buddikaram, the largest Cambodian Buddhist temple on the West Coast, is expected to draw people from all over the state. The Long Beach complex will eventually include a school, library, senior center, homeless shelter and Cambodian art depository. The first center to serve the war-ravaged Cambodian community, leaders are hopeful that it will help immigrants to heal past scars and to rebuild for the future. Most of the Cambodians, having been through the ordeals of war and genocide, bring with them an excruciating fear of earthquakes; they live in terror of another disaster that will take their loved ones from them. After the October 1, 1987 earthquake, about 2,000 Cambodians left Los Angeles County and resettled in Fresno and other communities inland.

Like most other newly-arrived immigrant groups, the Cambodians tend to cluster, but one group in the San Fernando Valley has arrived at a possibly unique solution to the foreignness of their new land. About 1,000 inhabitants of a Van Nuys apartment building have reorganized the complex into the likeness of a Cambodian village. Doors are always open; tasks, like laundry, are shared; and herbs and vegetables are grown in the courtyard.

ASIAN

While the first group of refugees who arrived in 1979 were well educated and could use their professional skills, later immigrants were bewildered by American culture and a strange language. But even though most come from small farming communities where there was no opportunity to attain business skills, many have managed almost miraculously with small businesses—often doughnut shops, which some see as very American. In 1988 about 80 percent of the Cambodian businesses around Long Beach sold doughnuts. Ted Ngoy, who arrived in 1975 with $2,000, parlayed his assets into 25 doughnut shops and millions of dollars, and has now branched out to hamburgers and tacos. The Cambodian community, which has revitalized central Long Beach (87 to 300 businesses in a year), is now looking toward businesses that will cater not only to Cambodians but to a cross section of the people in the area.

Cambodians in the Los Angeles area celebrate two major festivals. The New Year's Festival occurs around April 15 (lunar calendar) and the Festival of Ancestors, Pchum Ben, about the end of September.

■ Filipino

The Philippines, under American colonial rule from 1898, was granted independence in 1946. Since immigration restrictions were lifted for those who worked for the United States government for 15 or more years, many Filipinos (or Pilipinos) came to the States under this special law. The first Filipino settlement in Los Angeles was established in the 1920s and by 1980 the census reported almost 100,000 in Los Angeles County. The Filipinos who came in the 1920s and 1930s worked in canneries and on farms, and settled near the Civic Center in an area then known as Little Manila; the area, however, was destroyed by redevelopment, and the community moved to the Temple/Beverly area between Glendale and Rampart Boulevards. The immigrant population changed after World War II and particularly after 1970 when Filipinos who were well educated also settled in Los Angeles.

Today Filipinos are one of the largest Asian groups in the county and maintain a longer waiting list for immigrant status than any other ethnic group. They are also, according to the Los Angeles *Herald Examiner*, the wealthiest Asian community (a large number can afford to send their children to private Catholic schools). About 300 Filipino voluntary organizations in Los Angeles (up from 40 in 1952) reflect the large number of Philippine language and regional groups represented in the city (there are about 90 different languages spoken on the more than 7,000 islands that comprise the home country). Since the Philippines is the only country whose foreign nationals can serve in the American armed services, a large number are employed by the United States Navy. Many Filipino women work as nurses. The current county population is estimated at 350,000 and the majority (about 75 percent) are foreign-born. Projections indicate that there will be one million by the year 2000.

The northwestern regions of central Los Angeles house the largest concentration of Filipinos in the city, but there are also groups in Glendale, Eagle Rock, San Pedro, Wilmington, and West Covina. Since 1900, according to some old-timers, there has been a desire to officially declare the Temple/Beverly area "Filipino Town," but the City Council has not acted on the proposal since warring factions within the community cannot reach consensus on how they want the area defined. Even though the district now has about seven Filipino clinics, six Filipino law offices, four Filipino restaurants, three Filipino social service agencies, five Filipino youth gangs and two Filipino factions (reputed to have declared a truce), the area has never developed a visible center akin to Chinatown or Koreatown. Filipinos are in other ways not as "noticeable" as other Asian groups in the City—their fluency in English (the 1988 United Way Report notes, however, that "significant cultural differences exist between Pilipinos and mainstream Americans in their use of the English language"), familiarity with American culture and preponderance of Spanish surnames allows them to blend in more easily than other Asian immigrant groups.

The Philippine Heritage Festival is the community's most prominent event, with a parade as the main attraction; the whole is a demonstration of ethnic display and symbolism. In the Philippines the parade usually is held on the last Sunday in May—the May Festival of Flowers in honor of the Virgin. Menez and Montepio in *CityRoots Festival* describe it as "an outdoor procession of formally attired young women called *sagalas*, who represent important titles of the Virgin, such as 'Mystical Rose,' and the characters from a dramatization of the search for the Holy Cross (Santa Cruz) by Empress Helena and her son, Constantine. The *Santacruzan* tradition has been celebrated since 1979 in Los Angeles." Several months before the event, the organizer starts recruiting the *sagalas* from the young Filipinas who are chosen not only for their beauty but for their interpersonal skills, leadership, and social prominence. The main aspect of the festival is a parade, with the *Santacruzan* as the grand finale. Unlike the festival in the home country, which is primarily religious, in Los Angeles it serves cultural needs. The whole is primarily a showcase for the community and a symbol of its diversity; only second is it a symbol of devotion to the Virgin.

◼ Indian

The approximately 70,000 people of Indian descent in Southern California came in two waves. The earlier, in the 1960s and early 1970s, was composed mainly of students and professional people such as physicians and engineers. They came primarily from southern India, and were Tamilians, Kannadegas and Telugu-speaking peoples. Merchants from Gujarati in western India also began to arrive in the 1970s. The second group began coming in the late 1970s. These were in part the relatives of the professionals who had moved here earlier, and are those who opened shops and restaurants, forming the present energetic city-wide business class. Today the community has two bimonthly newspapers, each with 25,000 readers.

Indians have settled in many different areas of Los Angeles but there is a concentration in Cerritos, and Pioneer Boulevard in Artesia, is known as "Little India." The Artesia area, which has become one of the nation's largest Indian business districts (only Jackson Heights in Queens, New York and Chicago's Devon Street have more Indian stores and restaurants), has revitalized what was an aging business district on the Los Angeles-Orange County border. Today, these merchants, mainly Gujaratis, sell Indian sweets, appliances, groceries, clothing, jewelry and food to more than 12,000 Indian emigrees who live in the area and others who come to shop from as far away as the Bay Area and Phoenix. One lively entrepreneur, Moni Syal, combined the increasing demand for Indian food with the American "instant" hamburger and became the successful pioneer of Indian fast food.

While most Hindus worship at home where they have individual shrines, a spectacular Hindu Temple is being completed in Calabasas. Begun in 1981, the Sree Venkateswara Temple was consecrated in October 1987 and is the gathering spot for an estimated 10,000 Hindus in Southern California. The soaring, intricately carved towers and gold-tipped cupolas arise like a vision before those navigating the canyon road. The temple is as breathtaking as it is unexpected. Located on a four-and-a-half-acre site the temple was built almost entirely by Tamilian craftsmen known as *silpis* (each of whom must go through a grueling seven-year apprenticeship) who came from southern India to direct the building of the Temple according to strict guidelines set out in tenth-century religious documents known as the *Shastra*; "the dimensions of the shrine, the shape of the cupolas and the placement of the nine deities fit the rules laid down" in these documents. The Malibu Temple follows the Chola style, named after the Chola Dynasty (A.D. 900-1100) which some say gave India many of its greatest temple builders, and is the largest Hindu Temple of this style in the Western hemisphere. Kenneth J. Garcia in a Los Angeles *Times* article further notes:

> The mortar and brick walls are covered with intricate carvings of dragons, lions, elephants, idols and lotus blossoms. There is a central meditation hall, a multipurpose auditorium and nine domed towers encasing carved statues of the Hindu gods. Each statue was imported from India and installed by temple priests, who carefully decorate the deities with flowers and garments each day.

The three full-time priests put in days that begin at 6:00 A.M. and often continue well into the night.

Like other immigrant groups, Indians, over time, are making adaptations to their new land. The Indians in Los Angeles have become less overtly religious. Here, they do not have the means or the time to perform rituals properly and many have come to think of these traditional acts as un-American. Holy days are celebrated on the nearest weekend day rather than the day of occurrence; in India, many of these days would be holidays, but even if not, they would be celebrated on the day on which they fall. Traditionally, special cooks would prepare and leave food for the gods, but here the food is offered and then reclaimed.

As with other immigrant groups, things American are becoming important in the Indian community. Anniversaries, for example, which are of no consequence in India, are celebrated for the Temple with a *Puja* (worship). American education and American dress are taking over; married Indian women in Los Angeles generally cut their hair, a practice never seen in India since it indicates that the woman's husband will die. Arranged marriages, one of the most orthodox Indian traditions, are rapidly disappearing. The Los Angeles *Herald Examiner* quotes a City University of New York survey in which 49 percent of the Indians interviewed disapproved of arranged marriages and 46 percent disapproved of marrying exclusively within one's caste. Both of these conditions would be upheld by the orthodox in India. In the United States, however, because Indian communities are limited and scattered, there are numerous difficulties involved in finding an appropriate mate. Indians in Los Angeles have learned to compromise or even to completely disregard the customs of their ancestors. Even divorce, taboo according to Indian tradition, has become relatively common among Indian immigrants.

Indian Independence Day, celebrating India's independence from the British Empire in 1947, is celebrated in mid-August. Included are folk and classical dances, traditional music and food, and theme fashion shows, such as "Bridal Dresses of India."

■ Korean

There are probably between 200,000 and 300,000 Koreans in the Los Angeles area (about 340,000 in Southern California) and they are now one of the fastest-growing immigrant populations in the city. The community could total more than one million by the year 2000, according to an official at the Census Bureau. This is an astonishing increase from census figures of about 9,000 in 1970 and 60,000 in 1980.

Unlike the agriculturally-oriented Chinese and Japanese, the Koreans came to the United States primarily as businesspeople and, more than any other Asian group, have earned a reputation for entrepreneurship. The 1980 census indicated that 13.5 percent of all Koreans were then self-employed, which was the largest proportion of any immigrant group (possibly recently surpassed by Iranians). By 1982, Los Angeles had 25 percent of all Korean firms in the United States, the largest percentage in the country, and these businesses operated nearly five percent of all retail firms, although they comprised less than one percent of the population. Eighty percent of Koreans living in Los Angeles work in Korean-owned firms. The *Korean Directory of Southern California, 1986-7*, lists more than 8,000 Korean-owned businesses in the Los Angeles area. A special supplement of the Los Angeles Times, "The Koreatown News," was delivered to 300,000 homes in December 1988 encouraging advertisers to take advantage of the large number of Koreans in the area, whose median household income is over $37,000. And Koreatown (named such in 1980 in response to repeated requests from the Koreatown Development Association), concentrated on Olympic Boulevard between Normandie and Hoover, is now larger than Chinatown or Little Tokyo and houses about 33 percent of the Koreans in Los Angeles County. The area has been transformed into a prosperous, rapidly expanding business area. Koreatown Plaza is a $25 million, trilevel indoor mall, the largest project undertaken by Koreans in Southern California.

There are a number of factors which contribute to Korean successes. The underground banking system, or *kye*, is more pervasive and the clubs tend to be larger than their Chinese and Japanese counterparts. In a 1987 study Ivan Light of UCLA found that more than 36 percent of the Koreans surveyed said that at least part of their start-up capital came from a *kye*. The system unfortunately is beginning to be abused and the clubs may not be as effective in the future. This institution is so ingrained in Korean culture that a Koreatown bank has instituted a savings and loan plan along the lines of a *kye*. Korean success is also a result of a willingness to work long hard hours—up to 130 hours a week. Koreans often buy up businesses in run-down areas, begin by cleaning and restoring the dilapidated buildings, and then once the businesses are established include sub-businesses like lotto tickets and check cashing in order to turn a profit. Many are wonderfully adaptable, taking over such non-Korean enterprises as failing doughnut shops and Jewish delicatessens. Dying areas of the city are revitalized through this process, which also provides work for other immigrants. Korean prosperity, however, has not been obtained without friction. When Koreans opened stores in south central Los Angeles, there were major confrontations with the resident Blacks. The clash of cultures, and the language barrier, caused the Blacks to complain about their treatment as customers and the Koreans about their treatment as merchants. Robberies, violence and alleged murders were the result, but both sides have been working at resolving the conflicts.

The rapid growth of the Korean population has resulted in additional problems. To address the issues of Koreatown development, domestic violence, drug abuse and youth gangs, a conference of business executives and community leaders, called "Koreatown 2000," was held in December 1988. Lack of English and poor communication within families were cited as two of the most prominent problems within the Korean community. In addition, Koreatown, which now houses about a third of all Korean businesses in the county, was seen by some as too insular. Existing community problems tend to increase when there is no cultural center and little means to attract non-Koreans into the neighborhood.

Koreans in Los Angeles read four daily newspapers in Korean as well as four weeklies and bimonthlies; one of these, the *Korea Central Daily*, has a worldwide circulation of over two million. Another newspaper, in conjunction with the United States Embassy, organized in 1988 reunions between men in Los Angeles on temporary visas and their wives still in Korea. Some of these couples had not seen each other for six years. The wives (or in one case the husband) stayed for a month and then most returned to Korea to await the time when their spouses would have permanent visas.

At the Dharma Sah Zen Center (Korean Zen Buddhism) on Cloverdale Avenue near Park La Brea, practice stays close to that of Korean monasteries. The extremely regimented routine attracts more American practitioners than Koreans, since Koreans find it too demanding and Korean Americans are more likely to be Christian than Buddhist. In fact about 70 percent begin attending various Protestant churches as soon as they arrive—there are now about 500 Korean Protestant churches in Southern California—and it is these church groups that hold the communities together; they provide not only social and cultural activities but a place for making business connections. Church groups, for the Koreans, take the place held by clans and benevolent associations which exist for the Chinese and Japanese, but there is some question as to whether future generations will continue to find church groups important as social centers.

Since 1974 Koreatown has held its largest festival of the year in mid-September, centered around a large parade along Olympic Boulevard. The week-long cultural event includes folk-song and dance contests, a Tae Kwan Do exhibition, a calligraphy contest, a night of Korean literature, and *changtar* (a carnival and trading place). The floats are generally sponsored by corporations and display giant shoes or VCRs along with attractive young women in native costumes. In 1988 there were 20 floats seen by about 20,000 spectators; one float featured Miss Korea, and all of them celebrated the Olympic Games. The Games also provided the impetus for the first Korean-American float in the Rose Parade. Conceived to promote the Seoul Olympics, this float brought the Rose Parade to many Koreans in Asia for the first time.

■ Laotian

The Laotian population is difficult to evaluate; "Lao" never appears as a separate category for census counts and there is enormous diversity within the population (in Laos there are more than 68 different ethnic groups indicating the many peoples who have settled in the country over the years) with more than a dozen groups represented in California. The largest subgroup in Los Angeles County is the Lao (river valley dwellers); others include the Lao-Mien, Lao-Khmu and the Lao-Hmong (mountain dwellers).

A United Way report roughly estimates the Los Angeles County Lao population at about 30,000. Laotians tend, not surprisingly, to cluster by ethnic subgroup so that the entire Lao population appears widely distributed throughout the county. One group, the Hmong women, are beginning to find a place in the city; their textile arts are receiving critical attention and have been exhibited at the Woman's Building in downtown Los Angeles.

■ Pacific Islander

American Samoans (who are United States Nationals rather than immigrants) are the largest Pacific Island group in Los Angeles. There are at present more Samoans here, about 60,000, than in American Samoa. They came primarily because of the limited opportunities for education or careers in their home country. As many knew how to can fish, they gravitated toward the canneries on Terminal Island; most today live in Carson.

Samoan students in Los Angeles have attracted attention because of their abilities as football players, as the Mighty Colts of Carson High School. The large, muscular members of the team are watched carefully by college recruiters and enthusiastically followed by the entire school. The whole student body uses and understands Samoan cheers and half the football team wears *ie lavalas* (wrap skirts which are seen at various other places around town such as on gas station attendants). Opposing teams are reputed to be intimidated by just looking at the Colts. After a game in 1971, co-coach Gene Vollnogie recalls that "our Samoan guys did a victory dance called a *mele mele*. One player rubbed his hands together and kicked his legs in the air, and this guy had about 20 inch biceps. The other guys were all yelling 'Ah!Ah!' . . . all these pink-cheeked kids [on the other team] were all just standing there watching, with their eyes kind of wide. Their coach came over to me and said, 'If you'd have done that before the game, our guys wouldn't have even showed up.' "

Unlike most other Asian groups, Samoans tend not to be education- and business-oriented. They seldom attend college, and have a median Asian-family income higher only than that of the war-torn Vietnamese refugees. The reasons are both cultural and economic—what works in Samoa does not seem to be the "American way," and they have clung to the old ways more than most of the Asian groups now in Los Angeles. The traditional *matai* (chief) system, for example, persists, and these family leaders continue to make major decisions, to arrange significant family events and to arbitrate disputes.

The *matais* donned traditional garb at a four-day Samoan festival which began on August 31, 1988, to celebrate the independence of Western Samoa and the 88-year relationship between American Samoa and the United States. Traditional Samoan food and festivities were featured, as well as banana-paring and coconut-grating contests.

Among other Pacific Islander groups, the Hawaiian community, about 7,000, celebrates in July the Ho'olaulea Hawaiian Festival which features a king and prince. Events include the blowing of a shell horn, hula dance troups and traditional games. The Los Angeles Tongan community is estimated at about 20,000, the Guamanian at about 4,000; and there are small communities from Indonesia and Fiji.

■ Thai

Unlike the Chinese, Japanese, Filipinos, and Koreans, Thais have no bitter immigration history. They were not forced from their country by economic conditions but rather came seeking a novel life and greater educational opportunity. First generation Thais may arrive with a better understanding of English than most Asian groups, as in Thai schools English instruction begins in the early grades. Thais appear to be extremely adaptable, and many have opened restaurants in all areas of the county; these are of such quantity and quality that many Angelenos now frequent a local Thai restaurant along with their American coffee shop and Mexican taco bar.

Most Thais came here in the early 1970s. The United Way estimates about 100,000 Thais in the Los Angeles area, with the largest concentrations in the mid-Wilshire and Hollywood districts.

The traditional Thai New Year celebration begins April 13 with the three-day festival of Songkran. At North Hollywood's Wat Thai (Buddhist Temple), the Los Angeles Thai community gathers the weekend before April 13 to celebrate and feast. Events include ancestral blessings by the monks and Thai boxing.

■ Vietnamese

By 1970 the end of the Vietnam war had brought more than 60,000 Vietnamese, Laotian and Cambodian refugees to Los Angeles. The number of Vietnamese in the county has jumped from about 26,000 in 1980 to between 80,000 and 85,000 today, as the Vietnamese here sponsor and bring over relatives from Vietnam and refugee camps. (There is also a substantial population around Westminster in Orange County.) A United Way study indicates that the Vietnamese have the lowest median household income of all the Asians in the area ($9,610) and lack urban skills. Since 1975 and the fall of Saigon, many Vietnamese refugees have found their way to Lincoln Heights and the surrounding areas, where the Asian population has risen from about 5 to 40 percent. At Belmont High School in the Fall of 1979, 40 percent of new enrollees were Vietnamese boat people. The Vietnamese in Los Angeles (and all over the country) have a particularly difficult problem as they try to cope with the American attitudes regarding Vietnam veterans, who Americans do not see as including Vietnamese. Yet almost every Vietnamese in Los Angeles carries emotional and/or physical scars from the war.

The area's Vietnamese residents practice both traditional and western religions. America's oldest and largest Vietnamese Buddhist Temple, the Chua-Viet-Nam is in an old apartment building on the edge of Koreatown. A group of Catholic Vietnamese have repaid the church of St.Pius in Sante Fe Springs for relocating 54 Vietnamese families to Southeast Los Angeles by scraping together $12,000 and donating hundreds of hours of work to create an elaborate shrine of the Virgin. The Vietnamese, who comprise only ten percent of the parish, were organized by Pham Minh Thanh, who himself installed lights, water pumps for the fountain, and steel cables to hold the rocks together. At the dedication ceremony, which included hundreds of exploding fireworks, Thanh explained that "the devil is afraid of the noise and it is also a welcome."

A particularly well-known Vietnamese family in the city is the Vo, whose seven siblings can perform "thirty different programs of Vietnamese traditions lasting two hours or more." The Vos, while waiting eleven years for permission to leave Vietnam, deliberately set out to learn traditional Vietnamese music, dance, theater and martial arts from all areas of the country to save the culture that was being destroyed. They now perform in Los Angeles at New Years, birthday celebrations for deities, the birthday observation of the first king of Vietnam, the anniversaries of venerated figures, ceremonies honoring the ancestors, funerals, and Buddhist observances.

Irish Pub, Santa Monica

European

Small numbers of Western Europeans began arriving in Los Angeles before the middle of the nineteenth century, most of them adventurers attracted by new vistas. In the 1880s the Wicks Colony from Scotland and the Kingsbury Colony from England were founded in the Antelope Valley, and Palmdale was founded by German Lutherans. Europeans have arrived steadily and for a wide variety of reasons, but since their numbers tend to be moderate and their culture and appearance generally merge with that of White Americans they do not attract as much press or attention as Asians, Hispanics or Blacks. Their contributions, however, to the cultural and social life of Los Angeles are significant. Even European countries with small populations in Los Angeles, such as Luxembourg which has about one hundred citizens in the area, may retain a consulate.

Eastern Europeans, primarily Russians, have arrived throughout the twentieth century. While these communities here tend to be small—but with increasing numbers of Russian Jews due to *glasnost*—most have maintained a unique identity.

On a different note, it is perhaps inevitable that the land of Hollywood has over the years attracted European "nobility." The likes of Baron Frederick von Soosten, Prince Alessandro Tasca di Cuto and other marquises, countesses and baronesses have found a new life in Los Angeles. They live here, openly displaying their titles, despite the fact that in many countries without reigning monarchies—Germany, Austria and Italy for instance—the titles were legally abolished years ago.

■ Baltic

The Displaced Persons Act, which made it possible for refugees to enter the United States after World War II, favored the Baltic peoples—Latvians, Estonians and Lithuanians—because of their "nordic" appearance, reputation as hard workers, and high educational level. All three nationalities are represented in the Los Angeles area today with Lithuanians the most numerous. While each group maintains an independent identity and separate organizations, the Baltic peoples attend each others social and political functions and there is a Southern California Baltic Association; these peoples are drawn together by their common history as well as their intent for independence of the three homelands.

In a 1985 study of Lithuanian refugees in Los Angeles, Liucija Baskauskas notes that all informants remembered having arrived penniless. Twenty years later, almost all (except the unmarried and retired) either owned property or were members of a family that owned property. Many of the more than 15,000 Lithuanians in the greater Los Angeles area are in the professions, teaching, and real estate. They are dispersed throughout Los Angeles but there is a concentration in the Silver Lake-Glendale area which has the Lithuanian Catholic parish, community centers, publishing houses and restaurants.

Little is known about Lithuanians in Los Angeles before 1939, at which time there were 840. Most were of working-class background, and they organized the Lithuanian Worker's Union here. After World War II most Lithuanian immigrants were refugees from the Soviet Union and anti-Communist, and thus in conflict with the group already established.

Lithuanians continue to relocate to Los Angeles because of the now thriving community (this despite the fact that for most Lithuanians Los Angeles is the third place of relocation after coming to the United States). The Los Angeles community is growing, while others in the east and midwest are disappearing.

The Lithuanian community sponsors voluntary associations, youth festivals and cultural programs. Most activities are organized around the churches. The first, Saint Casimir, was established in 1941; in 1948 when it was enlarged, an elementary school, a rectory and a nunnery were added. There are large social gatherings called "Lithuanian Days" sponsored by the parish and by the central Lithuanian association. The largest, the Lithuanian Fair, is held at the church in early October and features folk dancing, singing and music, and craft demonstrations of weaving, egg decorating and the cutting of amber.

The community publishes a parish bulletin, a monthly local newspaper and a large international picture magazine. The major Lithuanian newspaper *Drauga*, published in Chicago, contains a regular section with news of Southern California Lithuanian Americans.

The Estonian Society of Los Angeles was initiated in 1929 and today organizes the Estonian Independence Day proceedings and social affairs for the community of about 800 people. The Community Center, Estonian House, was purchased in 1953. There is an Estonian choir, two folk dance troupes, a women's club and a senior citizens' organization.

The 3,000 Latvians in the Los Angeles area, like the other Baltic peoples, began to come here after World War II, attracted by the climate and the economic opportunites. This growing population sponsors the Latvian Association of Southern California, the Latvian Church of Southern California, a choir, a square dance group, a youth organization and an amateur theatre troupe.

■ Dutch

Dutch immigration to Southern California was at its peak around 1950, when the population was about 100,000. They began coming in the 1920s, but most arrived in the late 1940s when economic depression gripped Europe. Forty years ago a community of Dutch dairy farmers existed across what is now La Mirada, Cerritos, Norwalk, Bellflower, Artesia and Paramount. At that time the southeast area was the largest milk-producing region in California.

Today, the farmers have gone, but the Dutch influence, although slowly disappearing, remains. There are still tulip gardens, miniature windmills, drive-through dairies and business names like Rylaarsdam Realty and Dutch's Country Kitchen. There are also Dutch stores like the Holland-American Market and Import Co. in Bellflower, which stocks Dutch items ranging from frozen herring to wooden shoes, and the Artesia Bakery, which is run by sixth-generation Dutch bakers. Dutch social clubs are still in evidence, as is a newspaper, *The Holland News*, the only Dutch-language newspaper in the country.

 English

The English form one of the largest European groups in Los Angeles; approximately 100,000 immigrants in Southern California with about 250,000 second-generation. In Los Angeles they concentrate in Santa Monica; "We always gravitate to water," a consulate spokeswoman noted. The Santa Monica area boasts a number of "authentic" English pubs, and the Tudor House specializes in British take-out food. Social life is centered around clubs, which are generally in private homes, but the largest—The Mayflower—has its own building, where pantomimes are performed at Christmas.

Englishmen are reputed to have brought golf to Los Angeles, although few here apparently ventured the game before 1887 as it was considered un-American. After that, it caught on rapidly. According to L.L. Hill:

> . . . a few hardy souls, about 20 in number, finally sank some tomato cans in vacant lots centering around Pico and Alvarado and began teaching themselves the game. Overnight the sport became so popular that the Los Angeles Golf Club was formed and a larger plot of ground secured near the Rosedale Cemetery where a clubhouse costing $300 was erected . . . Before 1900 had arrived five other clubs had sprung up in as many neighboring cities so that on the initiative of Ed. B. Tufts and J. F. Sartori, charter members of the Los Angeles Golf Club, the present Southern California Golf Association was brought into being [The enthusiasm and the facilities escalated.] On this course on Washington's birthday, 1900, 29 contestants teed off in the qualifying round of the first tournament of the Southern California Golf Association. Thirteen years later, more than 100 teed off . . .

French

The earliest French settlers quickly found the common ground between France and California. The first Frenchman here, Louis Bouchette, established a vineyard on Macy Street around 1830. Louis (or Jean) Vignes, who arrived in Los Angeles in 1831, soon had the largest vineyard in California; he predicted that "California would one day rival France in the quality as well as the quantity of its wine," and had his vineyard's street (Vignes Street now in downtown Los Angeles) named in his honor. His nephew Jean Louis Sainsevain and brother Pierre are credited with making the first California champagne.

A sizeable number of French, mainly merchants, moved to Los Angeles at the beginning of the Franco-Prussian War (1870-1871) and a prosperous French colony developed around these merchants. The community was large enough that in 1883 a local French newspaper, *Le Progres*, was initiated. The French artist Paul de Longpre, as mentioned earlier, in 1901 traded three flower paintings for three acres of land at what is now the corner of Hollywood Boulevard and Cahuenga.

Today there are about 45,000 to 50,000 French nationals in Los Angeles who celebrate Bastille Day at the Triforium in mid-July.

■ German

The first German in Los Angeles, John Groningen (or Juan Domingo as he was known to the locals who had difficulty pronouncing his name), arrived on Christmas Day, 1828, when his ship was wrecked at San Pedro. He bought a large vineyard at the corner of First and Alameda streets and is said to have bought from the city the original site of Yang-na.

The Consulate General notes that there are today about 30,000 German Americans in Southern California who frequent 22 clubs in the Los Angeles area. A little of Germany can be experienced in Torrance, where the Alpine Village boasts 20 shops and a huge Munich-style beer hall. Oktoberfest takes place in the beer garden, and German Day is celebrated in August.

■ Greek

Greeks came to the United States in large numbers between 1900 and 1910, when famine drove many from their country. They also came to Los Angeles after the Second World War. Beginning with small businesses—like flower and vegetable stands—they built up larger ones or trained for the professions, becoming one of the wealthiest groups in the city. There is a daily Greek radio program, but no local newspapers.

The approximately 100,000 Greeks and Americans of Greek origin, are dispersed throughout the Los Angeles area as are Greek specialty stores and restaurants, but their cultural hub as well as their religious center, the magnificent Saint Sophia Greek Orthodox Cathedral, are found at Pico Boulevard near Normandie. The church, built in 1952 through the efforts of Charles Skouras, one of the first movie magnates, houses 17 crystal chandeliers, 12 immense stained glass windows, a painted tableau on the walls and ceiling (replaced inside the dome with Byzantine-style mosaics in 1989), and an aisle length of more than 150 feet. Other important Greek churches are St. Nicholas in Northridge and the Long Beach Assumption Greek Orthodox Church.

Major Greek festivals are associated with specific churches. The Feast of the Annunciation is celebrated March 25 at Saint Sophia and the Dormition of the Virgin at Long Beach. The Long Beach Assumption Greek Orthodox Church sponsors the Grecian Festival by the Sea on Labor Day weekend, where Greek dance, music, food and crafts are offered at the shore. The Blessing of the Waters is held aboard the Queen Mary on the Sunday following January sixth; in this rite, when the water is blessed a wooden cross is thrown into the sea, and young boys dive after it. The one who retrieves the cross is blessed by the bishop. A Greek festival, St. Katherine's, is held in early October in Torrance, and in September at the Greek Festival the entire grandstand area of the Santa Anita Racetrack is converted into a Greek marketplace/bazaar.

■ Gypsy (Roma)

Los Angeles has the country's largest Gypsy community, about 50,000 people. A true Fourth World nation—one without a country, like Native American peoples and the Inuit—they have been stateless since their movement from Northern India in the ninth century. Romani (or Romany), their language, is Indo-European, with Romanian, Hungarian and Slavic elements. With a long history of persecution, they came to the United States in large numbers at the end of the nineteenth century as refugees.

Today's urban Gypsies are not conspicuous; years of prejudice and prosecution have led them to hide their identity from outsiders, but the group preserves their traditions by keeping alive the language and customs. A Los Angeles *Times* article reports that Gypsies do a great deal more than tell fortunes, although that occupation is still practiced. They are also car salesmen, realtors, physicians and police officers. One is a cantor with a degree in Hebrew; another has a doctorate from London University's School of Oriental and African Studies. As a community they hold meetings at the Beverly Wilshire Hotel and the Rancho Park golf course.

Irish

The *Irish Cultural Directory for Southern California* tells us that there are more than one million people in Southern California who identify themselves as Irish by birth or descent. The directory also acquaints us with the Irish founding fathers of Los Angeles and the most well-known of its citizens, including Edward Doheny, the oil magnate, and William Mulholland, who was responsible for the design and building of the Los Angeles aqueduct.

Irish, over the past few decades, have been drawn to Los Angeles by job opportunities and the now substantial resident population; there were large bouts of immigration in the 1950s and the 1980s. American computer companies in particular, having become aware of the high standard of education in Ireland through the Industrial Development Authority (an Irish Government Agency in Santa Monica), have been recruiting at Irish Universities. The increasing population of Irish nationals has led the community to produce *The Irish Network*, a social and business directory aimed at the new Irish in the Los Angeles area.

The city's Irish (about 20,000 Irish-born) celebrate Saint Patrick's Day with a parade now held in Hollywood, but the most extensive Irish event is the Irish Fair and Music Festival in June, the largest Irish cultural festival on the West Coast. The stated purpose of the event is to educate the general population about the real Irish, steering it away from the Hollywood stereotype. Events include a horse show of Irish Connemara ponies which are brought from all over the country, a dog show featuring Irish wolfhounds, and a music festival which includes folk and ballad groups from the home country. One area at the fair features Gaelic plays and instruction in the Gaelic language, and at Tara village, participants dressed in period costumes reenact the life of an ancient Irish village.

The *Irish American Press* is a monthly newspaper published in Los Angeles, and the Irish Hour is heard Sunday afternoons on KIEV radio. The Irish Rover, a Santa Monica pub, is a popular meeting place for the Irish who live on the west side.

■ Italian

About 20,000 Italian Americans today live close to the harbor and in Los Feliz. The first Italian community was located in what is today Chinatown, where some of the old Italian restaurants like Little Joe's still remain. In general, the Italians here are so assimilated that we do not think of Italian restaurants or Italian food (pasta, pizza) as foreign.

Los Angeles' most famous Italian immigrant was surely Sabatino Rodia, the architect of what is known today as Watts Towers. The nine Towers, which range in height from 13 to 100 feet, are listed on the National Register of Historic Places and are a world-recognized attraction. They were constructed between 1921 and 1954 without scaffolding, welding torches or power tools; Rodia used a framework of steel rods and pipes which he wrapped and tied with iron mesh and wire, and then coated with mortar and decorated. The decoration consists of 70,000 sea shells and salvaged pieces of pottery, porcelain and glass—green from 7-Up bottles, blue from Milk of Magnesia bottles—plus bits of flower pots, dishes and tiles. Asked why he built the Towers, Rodia responded, "I had in mind to do something big, and I did."

■ Polish

In 1860 there were 720 Poles in California, about whom little is known. A small group which arrived about twenty years later, however, received a great deal of attention. This latter group was the one surrounding Madame Modjeska; its California story began in Cracow one evening in 1875 when Count Charles Bozenta Chlapowski and his actress-wife, Helene Modjeska, were entertaining a group of intellectual radicals bitter about the Russian takeover of their homeland. A plan to emigrate to America emerged from that meeting and the group of 11 eventually chose to move close to the German community in Anaheim, since they could converse in German. Their commune was modelled after Brook Farm (an 1840s experiment emphasizing plain group living and intellectual thought), and the participants included the author Henryk Sienkiewicz (*Quo Vadis*). Nonetheless, after about 18 months and a substantial outlay of funds, they decided that farming was not their forte. Madame Modjeska remained in America as a stage actress; the others returned to Poland. The sojourn of this group, albeit brief, was one of the earliest European settlements in Southern California.

The Los Angeles Poles were never concentrated in one area of the city and this dispersion slowed down the establishment of Polish parishes. Until the Polish Home was built on Avalon Boulevard in 1924 many Poles attended mass at St. Vibiana's Cathedral. The first Polish mass held in the new Home was celebrated by the reverend Bronislaw Krezeminski; services were held there until 1926. Various other locations were used until 1944, when the congregation purchased the estate of Fatty Arbuckle on West Adams Boulevard and created a chapel which served until money was available to build a church. Named Our Lady of the Bright Mount (Matka Boska Czestochowska), for the hill of the monastery of Czestochowa, which houses the revered ancient Dark Madonna of the Czestochowa icon, it was dedicated in 1956 as a national parish. The church houses a copy of the icon accurate to the twin sword slashes on the Virgin's cheek. In 1959 Guardian Angel Polish National Catholic Church was established, the only Polish National Church west of the Rockies.

A directory issued by the Polish community in 1950 indicated that at that time there were 30 Polish-American groups in Los Angeles, including Councils of the Polish National Association, Polish Women's Alliance, The Polish Literary and Dramatic Circle and the Polish University Club. A local newspaper, The *Panorama of Polonia*, is still published once a month. The national daily paper, *Dziennik Zwiazkowy*, distributed by the Polish National Association, has a weekly California edition providing news of interest for Los Angeles Poles.

■ Russian

There have been three waves of Russian immigration into Los Angeles from the U.S.S.R. (Armenians are discussed in a separate section). The first group left Russia after the revolution and arrived in Los Angeles around 1920; most went first to Europe or China and made their way to America from there. In 1940 there were about 25,000 Russians in Los Angeles. Large numbers resided north and south of Brooklyn Avenue from State street to the City boundary.

The second group consisted of people displaced during the Second World War; many had been taken to Germany as workers and never returned to Russia. Like other ethnic groups where factions have dissimilar backgrounds, the Russians in Los Angeles tend to have conflicting ideas and interests. Those who left Russia in 1920 are reputed to be more genteel but also more snobbish than those who left after World War II, and have some difficulty accepting the latter.

A third wave of immigration from Russia consists of the more than 20,000 Soviet Jews who began to arrive around 1970, and are still coming in relatively large numbers. (The Jewish community from Russia, which came earlier to Los Angeles, includes those who live in the Venice area of Los Angeles. This group is not Russian-speaking and is today dying out.) Whereas in the U.S.S.R. "Jewish" is considered a nationality, here the language of the Soviet Jews labels them as Russian; in most cases these people have never before considered themselves Russian, a situation which must cause them considerable confusion on their arrival. About 2,000 were expected to arrive in 1989, which now makes Southern California home to more Soviet Jewish emigrees than any American city except New York. (To accomodate the large numbers leaving Russia due to new Soviet policy, the American quota for Russian refugees was raised in January 1989.) As the city's funds for refugee assistance has dropped sharply, Jewish and city organizations are struggling to raise the money needed to help these newcomers settle, find jobs and learn English.

Many Soviet Jews settle (at least at first) in the Fairfax/West Hollywood area where Russian-Jewish stores, such as Gastronom, are clustered. Older Russian emigres resent the attention lavished on the Jews and see the newer arrivals as "Soviet," despite the fact that all emigres left for political reasons and define themselves as anti-Soviet (that is, anti-Communist). In addition, all tend to be politically and religiously conservative (the more religious Jews usually chose to settle in Israel rather then the United States). The Soviet Jews often find they have little in common with American Jews, and therefore seek out the company of other Soviet Jews. Elderly men hold religious services led by rabbis who operated underground in the Soviet Union, and all display their Soviet roots by tossing back vodka and herring after morning services. They publish a small newspaper for the Soviet Jewish community.

The 5,000 Russian immigrants in West Hollywood—most elderly Jews—tend to be insular, learn no English and find it difficult to adjust to a free society. The community, however, is reaching out to them. Zigmund Vays, the only Russian immigrant to serve on any of the city's boards since West Hollywood was incorporated four years ago, persuaded the city to spend $50,000 to establish a Russian Cultural Center. The center now offers English language classes to the Russians (and Russian classes to Americans), instructs the new immigrants in the mysteries of American life—such as checkbooks and push-button phones—and offers a series of cultural events. Elected officials are invited to help the immigrants learn about civic responsibilites. In contrast to the West Hollywood group, however, are the assimilated and successful medical professionals who are concentrated in West Los Angeles.

The Christian Russian community has always been spread around the city. Russians in Los Angeles do not cluster around their churches as the Greeks tend to do. The oldest of the three Russian Orthodox churches in the city is the Holy Virgin Mary Cathedral, built in 1928 on Michel Torena Boulevard in Silver Lake. A true Los Angeles product, its design was based on that of the church which appeared in the movie The Cossacks.

The Molokane or "Holy Jumpers," an extremely private religious sect which split off from the Russian church in the seventeenth century, now make their home in East Los Angeles.

Many Russians in Los Angeles before World War II were connected with the movie industry as artists, seamstresses and costume designers. A people who tend to acculturate quickly professionally if not socially, the community today is well educated and economically successful. A weekly newspaper in Russian, the Panorama, combines Los Angeles emigre news, and literary and cultural offerings. There is also a Russian-language telephone directory.

■ Scandinavian

There are more than 100,000 Scandinavian Americans in Los Angeles County. Norwegians are the largest group, with the second largest Norwegian community in the United States after Minneapolis, but there are also concentrations of Danes, Swedes and Finns, and about 200 Icelanders. There is no one Scandinavian area of the city, but there is an old Norwegian community in San Pedro and a Finnish cluster in the San Fernando Valley. As with many other immigrant groups social life tends to be centered around clubs.

The old Norwegian community in San Pedro is the most cohesive. Established more than 80 years ago its center is the Norwegian Seaman's Church and associated shops. The major holiday, Constitution Day on May 17, is celebrated with a large street party. The Swedes celebrate Midsummer Eve and Day at Wasa Park in Azusa and Lucia Day on the 13th of December.

Scots

The first Scot to settle in the area, James (Santiago) McKinley, arrived in Los Angeles in 1831. Hugo Reid, who arrived soon after in 1834, set himself up in business and married Victoria, daughter of the chief of the Gabrielinos (the local Native American people). Reid, who became a politician, is best known for writing a series of articles in 1852 for the Los Angeles *Star*, which described in detail the language, government, religion, food, dress, medicine, customs, sports, traditions, legends, and missionary life of the original natives of Los Angeles County.

Scottish Americans in Los Angeles have for over 50 years held an Annual Scottish Festival, officially known as The Highland Gathering and Festival, which has met every Memorial Day weekend for the past several years at the Orange County fairgrounds in Costa Mesa. Ten thousand people from the United States and Canada compete in traditional games, such as tossing the caber (a heavy wooden pole) and throwing the hammer; games for children; and dances and music—bagpipe bands compete for trophies and prizes.

■ Yugoslav

There are about 30,000 Yugoslavs in the San Pedro area. Most are Croatian, about half from the town of Komiza on the island of Viz. Influential in the development of the Los Angeles fishing industry, Croatians began the Starkist and Van Kamp seafood companies. The Yugoslavian community is split along Croat and Serb lines, with a further split between those Croats who wish to return to an independent Croatia and those who wish to remain in the United States. Most of the approximately 10,000 Serbs are employed in heavy construction, and had a major role in the construction of the Los Angeles Freeway system.

A Croatian Festival is held at the Alpine Village in July, and an Autumn festival is held at St. Sava Serbian Orthodox Church in San Gabriel.

Saint Sophia Greek Orthodox Church,
Los Angeles

The Islamic Center of Southern California, Los Angeles

Middle East

The political boundries of the peoples of the Middle East are often not as clear-cut as in other parts of the world. A number of peoples from countries including Egypt, Iran, Israel, Jordan, Saudi Arabia and Soviet Armenia are discussed in this section using a geographical basis for defining the area rather than a political one.

■ Arab

There are between 200,000 and 300,000 Arabs and Arab Americans living in Los Angeles, which is the second largest Arab population in the United States. They come because of the climate, the economic potential and the ethnic diversity of the area and have settled in many parts of the city—including Glendale/Arcadia/ Pasadena/Burbank, Long Beach/Palos Verdes, Torrance, Northridge and adjacent areas— but do not concentrate geographically in terms of native country. The middle class, mainly shopkeepers, are found primarily in the Hollywood area, along with Armenian and other Middle Eastern groups. Arabs have purchased aircraft and technological expertise from the aerospace industry but Arab investment in the city is not high compared to that of groups like the Japanese, British and Canadians.

The News Circle Publishing Company, founded in Los Angeles in 1972, publishes a monthly magazine for Arab-Americans called *The News Circle*, which concentrates on news from the Arab homelands and about the Arab community in Los Angeles. Also published by News Circle is the *Arab American Almanac*, a 322-page reference book for Arab Americans all over the country, now in its third edition (almanac is an Arabic word meaning weather or state of condition). Listings include national, regional and local organizations, religious institutions, a country-wide list of press and media, a state-by-state directory and a literary bibliography. There are chapters on the "History of the Arab-American community" and "Arab contributions to Western Civilization." The company also publishes *The Mideast Business Guide*. Other Los Angeles organizations produce newspapers, and television (channel 18) and radio programs. Members of each Arab nation tend to gather to celebrate the Independence Day of their country.

■ Armenian

Los Angeles County, with about 250,000 Armenians (most in Hollywood and Glendale), is the largest Armenian population outside the homeland and supports 11 schools, 16 churches and a wide range of organizations. Despite the fact that the community was shaped during the 1960s, large numbers continue to arrive in the city (13,000 in 1988). The commitment of those here to those in the home country was evident after the December 1988 earthquake in Soviet Armenia; millions of dollars were raised in only a few days. The amount of money raised also indicates the success of some members of the population. When George Deukmejian ran for California Governor in 1982, more than 20 percent of his campaign financing came from Armenians. Overall, however, this is a divided community where new arrivals often claim they are discriminated against by their more settled countrymen.

As Soviet officials quietly began (under the new Russian policy regarding emigration) approving thousands of exit visas, Los Angeles County officials became aware that they were totally unprepared for the large numbers of Armenians who were arriving in the city, since unlike the Southeast Asian community, whose large numbers are aided by a well-established network of private agencies, the Armenian community has been virtually bereft of such groups. The major problem has been attributed to the federal government, which has been increasing refugee admissions but at the same time radically decreasing funding to local agencies for refugee assistance. Social services and schools scramble to make do with too little money, too few translators and too little space. The most pressing needs, in addition to funding, are providing English classes and finding housing. The city in the past has never received advance notice that refugees are on their way, and usually the first indication of an additional Armenian presence is when the new arrivals show up at school to register their children. Most of the recent refugees are factory workers and most arrive destitute. A new United States policy was announced in August of 1988 stating that the blanket refugee status accorded Soviet and Eastern bloc immigrants will give way to individual determinations of refugee status, since the State Department does not have the budget to cover expenses; from

October 1987 to August 1988 the State Department issued $14 million for Soviet-Armenian immigrants.

With their widely varying backgrounds, homelands and religions, it is not surprising that the Armenian community is not cohesive. Those here are split between two major political parties and numerous smaller factions. Armenians from places other than the Soviet Union criticize their fellows for "deserting the homeland." They have been unified only by the genocide (the 1915 Armenian massacre in Turkey) and each year on April 24th, the entire Armenian community congregates in Montebello to remember the event.

Different groups have settled in various parts of the city. Armenians from the Russian Empire, who were in Los Angeles relatively early, originally settled in Montebello. As this group became affluent due to a well-organized trash-collecting business, most moved to Pasadena and other wealthy areas. The Turkish (mainly from Istanbul) Armenians live in Glendale and Pasadena, the Iranian Armenians mainly in Glendale, and the Egyptian Armenians, who came in the 1950s, are spread around the city, as are the Lebanese Armenians, reputed to be the most adaptable and enterprising. As with most immigrant groups, those who have been here longest tend to be the most dispersed—third- and fourth-generation Armenians have moved to the beach cities and Inglewood, where more frequently English is being used in the Armenian church. One group is trying to buy a large parcel of land in the Hollywood Hills, part of which would be occupied by an Armenian church.

Soviet Armenians have tended to migrate to East Hollywood, where a section with more than 50,000 Armenian inhabitants is known as "Little Armenia." At Ron's Market, huge blocks of pistachio halvah sit alongside whole dried veal tongues. At Hye ("Armenian") Plaza there is an Armenian optics store, Armenian butcher shop and an Armenian art gallery, and at the Sassoon Club the Soviet emigres, who arrived here as young men in their mid-20s and grew up without finding a viable niche in American society, sit, smoke and sip Turkish coffee. "Fashion of Europe" is an all-Armenian shopping center on Hollywood Boulevard.

The large numbers of Armenians in the city prompted the Los Angeles City Department of Cultural Affairs and Councilman Michael Woo to sponsor the first Armenian Cultural Festival at Barnsdall Park in October of 1986. This event has become annual, and in 1988 3,000 members of the Armenian community attended. A variety of Armenian music and dancing was accompanied by stuffed grape leaves, *beurak* (pastry) and *tahn* (yogurt and water). The increasing population is also reflected in the 1987 *Armenian Directory* (in Armenian and English), then in its eighth year of publication, which runs over 300 pages. During the 1960s the two major newspapers, which had started in Fresno, relocated to Los Angeles. By the late 1960s the first Armenian schools, including a high school in East Los Angeles, had been established as well as an Armenian theater group, a choral group and an Armenian allied art association. In 1965, a monument to the genocide was dedicated in Montebello. The established Armenian community has created a large and secure environment here, but the new arrivals are faced with the difficulties of all immigrant peoples with few resources.

In the mid-1970s a large number of Armenians arrived from Lebanon, Soviet Armenia and Iran. The Soviet Armenians were so well prepared for their relocation, through conversations and letters with friends and relatives already in Los Angeles, that many of them knew exactly where they wanted to live and in which stores they wanted to shop. Those from Soviet Armenia continue to pour into Los Angeles County. As a result of Mikhail Gorbachev's *glasnost*, 1988 saw the arrival of about 13,000 emigres to Los Angeles, about 90 percent of those who had come to the United States. According to Councilman Michael Woo this is "the single largest influx of any ethnic group since the resettlement of the Vietnamese boat people in the late 1970s." Most are expected to settle in Hollywood and Glendale.

The Armenian community sponsors two newspapers in English—the *Armenian Observer* and the *California Courier*—and up to ten others in Armenian. In early 1988 Shagen Arutyunyan, a Soviet dissident who spent eight years in a prison camp, his wife and four fellow Soviet Armenian emigres founded *Yerkoonk* or "Birthpains," a monthly newspaper that they write, edit and paste up in the living room of Arutyunyan's apartment. There are Armenian television (Channel 18) and radio programs; "Happy Harry," an Armenian host, is on KTYM radio every weekend morning.

The United States Armenian population in general has been noted as a particularly literate one (it is said that more books are published per capita in Soviet Armenia than any other region in the world), and those in Los Angeles publish the *Armenian Review*, a scholarly periodical, and *Ararat*, a literary journal. Abril, an Armenian bookstore, is on Santa Monica Boulevard near Western Avenue.

■ Iranian

In the early 1970s there was no Iranian community in Los Angeles. By the late 1970s, however, the beginning of the Ayatollah Khomeini's reign had started millions on their flight from the country. Between 300,000 and 400,000 (20 percent of the total number in the United States) found their way here and today the Los Angeles Iranian business directory covers more than 800 pages. This largest concentration in the United States includes members of all four Iranian religious groups—Muslims, Baha'is, Jews and Christians (Armenians). Muslims, although dominant in the home country, are a minority here—Muslims who leave home are by definition not highly religious.

Most of the immigrants are well educated—about half have graduate degrees (many from California colleges)—and are well-off, the cream of Irani society who could afford to relocate. Most have urban roots; about 60 percent are from Teheran. Iranian Jews, on the other hand, usually come in as refugees.

Many have been successful in their relocation—some admirably so, such as the Mahboubi family who developed the Rodeo Collection in Beverly Hills, and the three men who built the Adray's chain. A good deal of Iranian money has been invested in Beverly Hills (Farsi is commonly heard in the Beverly Hills school system these days), Westside and San Fernando Valley real estate. The approximately 20,000 Iranis who work downtown have transformed the garment district—one alley in the area is described as "a Middle Eastern bazaar"—and rejuvenated the jewelry area. Other Iranians in Los Angeles are running kosher butcher shops, solemnizing marriages, and serving as calligraphers and astrologers. Still others are working long hours and holding onto a dream. One Armenian Irani, a former accountant, has been driving a taxi while trying to assemble $150,000 to buy a gas station.

Some of the Irani media has simply been shifted to Los Angeles. Pari Mirhashem-Abasalti now publishes her *Rahe-Zendegi* ("Way of Life") magazine from Westwood rather than Teheran, and an Iranian news commentator can be heard on cable television every morning. There are also locally-produced Iranian radio programs, a second Farsi magazine and six Farsi newspapers.

Professional Iranian classical musicians, some well-known in the home country, have resettled in Los Angeles, as have musicians interested in popularizing or "westernizing" Persian music. The preferred setting in

Iran for playing "serious" Iranian music was at private homes, but in Los Angeles Iranian nightclubs provide the musicians with their major opportunity to work.

■ Israeli

There are between 100,000 and 200,000 Israelis in the Los Angeles area. They live in all parts of the county, but concentrations are found in the Fairfax district, on the Westside and most notably in the San Fernando Valley where hundreds of Israeli businesses have been established. In all of these areas they join concentrations of the larger Los Angeles Jewish community (500,000 to 600,000, the second largest Jewish community in the United States after New York).

Many Israelis have settled here since the mid-1980s. The immigrants who find their way to Los Angeles (or more generally those who leave Israel) are by definition among the least religious of those in the home country; they are often young people who visit after serving in the army and then decide to stay, or well-educated professionals with young families who come with money and establish businesses or professional careers. Most do well here.

Two weekly newspapers, *Israel Shelanu* and *Hadshot L.A.*, are published in Los Angeles, and an Israeli radio program, "Galay L.A.," is heard on KFOX-FM Tuesdays and Sundays. There is an Israeli music store, an Israeli barbershop and Israeli banks. The community also supports a number of service and cultural organizations including the Israeli Organization of Los Angeles, which promotes activities in the area, and L.A. Hit, an Israeli theater and music group.

A recently-formed organization is the Commission on Israelis (a branch of the Council on Jewish Life), which attempts to involve Israelis in all aspects of the Jewish community and to educate the local Jews as to why Israelis are here. Some Jews, many of whom support the state of Israel, fail to understand why they are contributing to a country whose residents are leaving. In addition, the native Angelenos resist helping these newcomers to integrate, reasoning that if the Israelis become established, they will be less likely to return home. The Israelis on their part are ambivalent about being here, many feeling that they had to leave home because of the shortage of jobs (particularly in the electronics industry) or the pressures of psychological trauma. Assuming that they will one day go back, Israelis live with one foot in each world, integrated into neither. The result is a people who continue to feel like outsiders, and their children—who are not given the opportunity to receive a Jewish education and thus determine an identity—suffer the most. These Israelis, who did not belong to synagogues in the home country, tend not to join one here, particularly as they feel that their stay is temporary. Most, however, do make Los Angeles their permanent home, and because they stay, the Commission was organized in the early 1980s as a response to the growing problems.

■ Palestinian

It is difficult to know how many Palestinians there are in Los Angeles because so many carry passports from the country in which they were born, but Nadia Saad Bettendorf of the Arab American Anti-Discrimination Committee (ADC) estimates the total at between 40,000 and 50,000. She explains Palestinian history in the city:

> Palestinians really began coming to Los Angeles after the June 1967 war. . . . The Lebanese Civil War in 1975 increased the flow, and still more came during the 80s when jobs became less readily available in Arab states. People came to go to school or start businesses. Many went into merchant-service work like owning gas stations or grocery stores or sandwich shops. And there are also many lawyers, pharmacists, doctors and teachers within the community as well.

Many of the Palestinians here are Christians.

The Palestinian community has not settled in one area of the city, as they have had to follow available work and housing. Life in Los Angeles is difficult for many and Bettendorf further notes that "political, cultural and economic factors here are forcing them back [home]."

Son of the Kumase Asantehene at the
Coronation of the Los Angeles
Asantehene, Culver City 1987

African

Africans collectively do not comprise a large population in Los Angeles. For the entire state of California the 1980 census reports about 16,000. The breakdown is Nigeria, 3,300; Ethiopia, 1,200; Cape Verde, 360; Ghana, 360; other subSaharan, 2,410; and 1,060 from South Africa. These figures, however, seem incomplete. A spokesman for The Kenyan consulate, for example, indicated in August of 1987 that there were approximately 1,000 Kenyans in Los Angeles County. The Ghanaian community estimates that there are 1,500 here (including students) and the Ethiopian population is about 20,000. There are also small numbers from Somalia, Mali, Senegal, Tanzania, Uganda, Zimbabwe and likely other countries as well. The Nigerian community, one of the largest, is comprised mainly of Ibo and Yoruba peoples, the latter a large enough group that Yoruba is an official Los Angeles County court language. There are also small numbers of Kanuri and Hausa.

The Ethiopian community includes both members of the upper classes and destitute refugees. In June of 1988, Ethiopian Cultural Week was held in Los Angeles. Events included sales and entertainment at West Wilshire Park, art gallery shows, a fashion show and entertainment on the south lawn of City Hall.

The Asante of Ghana provide, no doubt, the most dramatic transplanted African ceremony in Los Angeles. On October 10, 1987, at the Culver City Veterans Auditorium, the first Los Angeles Asantehene (king of the Asante) was installed. The King of the Asante nation, the Asantehene (who resides in Kumase, Ghana), visited New York in 1985 and gave his blessing for the installation of a New York King. The New York Asantehene promised to bring together the Asante in other cities and influenced those in Los Angeles to begin organizing. This organization (there are about 200 Asante in the Los Angeles area) has stated that:

> as people from Ghana, we have a unique culture that should not be forgotten [and] we should be responsible for implementing

our cultural awareness programs in America, and for conveying our culture and traditions on to our children and to the generations to come. To be effective in this endeavor, we have to organize.

In addition, the Ghanaians in general felt that an organization would assist them to help Ghanaians still at home. To these ends, the Los Angeles community felt that the presence of a local Asantehene would be most effective.

Nana Osei Tutu Appiah was chosen by the local Asante elders and crowned in a traditional ceremony involving the installation of the Tribal Elders for the State of California and the unveiling of the "Golden Stool" of the Asante people. The Culver City auditorium was transformed by hundreds of dazzling Ghanaian robes, substantial gold jewelry and emblems of office, and large umbrellas covering those of high rank. The Asante came from all over the country—from New York, Miami and Chicago—and from the home country came the son of the Kumase Asantehene. The money for the elaborate ceremony was raised from monthly dues, tickets sold at the door and a grant from the Cultural Affairs Department of the City of Los Angeles. The festivities began in the early evening and continued into the small hours of the morning, as music and dancing followed the installation. The Los Angeles Asantehene came here in 1972 as a college student in engineering and now works for a local company as an electro-mechanical engineer. An Asante Cultural Day is celebrated the first weekend of October recreating events—marriages, installations of chiefs, village games—of the homeland.

Nana Osei Tutu Appiah and other Asante participate every year in the Kwanza parade, part of the Kwanza celebration held from December 26 to January 1. Modelled after the African harvest festivals, Kwanza is now honored by many Black Americans who are attempting to reclaim African traditions. The word is a shortened version of the Swahili expression *matunda ya kwanza*, meaning "first fruits," as Africans traditionally come together to celebrate the harvest of first crops. Singing, dancing and feasting are thought to aid spiritual growth and regenerate communal ties. The celebration was first held in Los Angeles in 1965, conceived by Black activist Maulana Karenga. In 1987 about 200,000 Blacks participated in Kwanza activities (about 10 million across the nation).

As initiated by Karenga, there are seven principles to the Kwanza celebration, with each day marking a different theme—self-determination, faith, creativity, unity, collective work and responsibility, and cooperative economic purpose. Altars (in 1987 set up in the Los Angeles Children's Museum) include straw mats (*mikeka*) symbolizing historical foundations, on which are placed a candleholder (*kinara*), symbolizing African ancestors and having seven candles representing the seven principles, and a cup (*kikombe*), symbolizing the unity of African peoples.

Entrants in the Kwanza parade, held along Crenshaw Boulevard to Leimert Park, dress according to the year's theme; entries include individuals wearing African masks and gowns, marching bands, drill teams, drum corps, youth groups, car clubs, and Black celebrities. In 1987, floats were entered by local colleges. At the park, traditional African costumes and masks appear. Many events associated with the ceremony, including a jazz caravan and private family observances, are held in various places around the city.

An African Heritage Festival is held early in May, featuring the dance, music, art and food of African peoples. On Memorial Day weekend, Africa Liberation Day highlights cultural expressions—poetry, song, dance, drumming—as a tribute to the liberation struggles of Africans. The lively African Marketplace takes place on the third weekend in July, August and September at the James H. Whitworth Park (moved from the William Grant Still Community Arts Center in 1989). A Yoruba priest leads the blessing that inaugurates the two-day event and chants to the ancestral spirit guides. At the Community Arts Center the back yard and the adjoining alleyway became a noisy, colorful bustle of song, dance, storytelling and tables piled with African arts, textiles and food. A visitor from New England noted, "I havn't seen this in Connecticut. You get a lot of fife and drums in Connecticut."

Santeria, an ancient religion from Nigeria that shares its roots with voodoo, is active in Los Angeles. Brought by Yoruba slaves to the New World between the sixteenth and nineteenth centuries, the religion has survived by secretly identifying Yoruba deities, known as *orishas*, with Catholic saints who represent similar virtues. *Santeria* is Spanish for "worship of saints" and the priests, known as *santeros*, are said to possess *ache*, the magical power of the saints. The core of the believers in Los Angeles are Cubans but there are a growing number of converts among African Americans, and other Caribbean and Latin American nationals. There are probably between 50,000 and 100,000 believers in Southern California. (Worldwide it is a religion with 75 to 100 million followers.) In Nigeria, there are public temples, but in Los Angeles the priests generally operate out of their homes or in the back rooms of *botanicas*, the shops that sell religious goods. Unless one seeks out a service, the *botanicas* are the most visible aspect of the religion. Three of the largest are located at the east end of Silver Lake—El Monte, Botanica El Indio and Botanica El Negro Jose.

According to the Los Angeles *Times*, African clothing and jewelry are becoming increasing popular with Black Americans. Stores that specialize in African imports report an upsurge in sales of traditional African dress as well as in the demand for contemporary clothes made of African fabric. The African Beat, a three-hour program of traditional and contemporary African music, can be heard on KCRW radio Saturday afternoons.

African Marketplace, Los Angeles

Australian Store, Los Angeles

"Invisible" Immigrants

Australians, New Zealanders, South Africans and particularly Canadians constitute the "invisible" immigrants. They look, act, and (in the case of Canadians) sound so much like Americans that they assimilate easily, and tend not to congregate in specific areas.

There are 5,000 to 10,000 Australians in Los Angeles County, with several thousand more in Orange County, where many Australian companies (most of the 350 major Australian businesses in the Los Angeles area are branches of the home office) are located. The majority of Australians are here because they work for American companies or are married to Americans. Australians have been touted as the most "travelled" people in the world and their young people (who used to visit England as the "finishing touch" to their education) today generally visit the United States; some stay and make their homes here. Unlike the British (with whom they are wont to compare themselves), Australians tend to be drawn together by events—Australian films or concerts, or parties in private homes—rather than places, such as pubs. There are also approximately 1,000 to 1,500 New Zealanders in the Los Angeles area, and like the Australians they are primarily professional and business people.

South Africans here are difficult to enumerate; an educated guess puts between 5,000 and 10,000 in the greater Los Angeles area, with additional significant communities around Irvine and in San Diego County. Many are Jewish. They are the only group of "invisible" immigrants who generally leave their homeland because of the political situation. Over the past 25 years (and with increasing frequency over the past 10 to 15) there has always been an exodus from South Africa at times of heightened racial conflict; large numbers of professional people, for example, left after the 1976 riots. Professional and economically successful individuals have always been more likely to emigrate and in recent years more of the monied have left the country. They are a people who, in general, seem to adapt quickly to life in Los Angeles, and to become involved in the community.

Canadians are much more numerous. Los Angeles, according to the Public Affairs Division of the Canadian Consulate, is the third largest Canadian city (after Toronto and Montreal and before Vancouver), housing 800,000 to one million Canadians in the greater Los Angeles area. They are an integral part of all facets of Los Angeles life, although most Angelenos would have difficulty differentiating them from Americans. Canadians, as well, although certainly always aware of their origins, usually do not feel foreign in the United States (the term "Canadian American" is never used); only a small percentage seek out Canadian events such as the celebration of Dominion Day on July 1. There are many in the film industry, in banking and in service industries. Canadian real estate holdings in the area are substantial.

United States Migrants

Native Americans (the now commonly accepted name for those formerly known as "Indians") and most Blacks (African Americans) are not immigrants. Native Americans, of course, are the only groups throughout the country who have never been immigrants, and many Blacks can trace their American ancestry back through five or six generations. Because of the circumstances of their histories and their appearance and because in some ways they define themselves as units, they are usually seen as ethnic groups. As migrants to Los Angeles (most have come here from other parts of the country) they have made unique and rich contributions and are an integral part of the Los Angeles story.

■ Native American ("Indian")

Geri Keams, an actress and filmmaker raised on the Navaho reservation, used to get up early every morning and make "a corn pollen offering as a thanksgiving to the sun and the earth" because taking care of and respecting the land is as important to her as to her ancestors. Attitudes toward the land are but one of the factors that make living in Los Angeles difficult for the Native American Community.

The 1980 census indicated that over one hundred of the 493 federally recognized Native American groups in the United States were represented in Los Angeles. Native American groups think there are closer to 200. Officially, the Los Angeles Native American community nearly doubled in the decade between 1970 and 1980—from 25,000 to 48,000 (plus 389 Inuits [formerly called Eskimos] and 497 Aleuts)—but a source at the American Indian Resource Center thinks this figure far too low. The Center's information indicates that there are about 70,000 Native Americans in Los Angeles County. Native American activists, according to the the Los Angeles *Times*, think that there are at least 200,000 in the County at any one time, most seeking economic opportunities. Whatever the numbers, the vast majority have come from other parts of the country—only one percent of the Los Angeles Native American population are descended from California Natives.

There are a number of reasons why Native Americans are such a difficult group to count. Many are transients, and many others have Spanish surnames and get included with Hispanics for census purposes. Unlike most other immigrants and migrants Native Americans do "go home again"; that is, back to the reservation. More than half of the elderly return home where they have free hospitalization, federal housing subsidies and food allowances. Young people return to the reservation if things do not go well, while others come and try their hand in the city. The result is that the Native American population in Los Angeles is one that "floats." Native Americans are not a cohesive group, and they do not live in the city as one. As members of many different nations they practice a large number of different traditional customs and speak a diverse number of languages. All Native Americans born in the United States since 1924 hold dual citizenship—they are both citizens of a Native American nation and the United States.

The Navaho are the largest group in the city; there are also Luiseño, Cherokee, Mattaponi, Sioux, Apache, Aleut, Cheyenne, Winnebago, Blackfeet, Gros-Ventre, Gabrielino, Seminole, Laguna, Shoshone, Comanche, Chumash, Paiute, Pomo, Huron and others including "enough members of the six Iroquois Nations [Seneca, Cayuga, Onondaga, Oneida, Mohawk and Tuscarora] around Los Angeles for them to hold their own social dances." Thousands of Native Americans came to Los Angeles between 1952 and 1980 on a Bureau of Indian Affairs program which was organized to "bring Indians into the mainstream of American life—i.e. 'relocation'."

Because Native Americans do not form a unified group and because the community is not a stable or centered one, these peoples tend to have more problems than many other groups. Their difficulties tend to be perpetuated since Native Americans fail to conform to generational adaptations. They are too few, too scattered and too diverse to even have a ghetto; in Los Angeles there is no Native American center. Children have low self-esteem; there is nowhere to go, no one to tell them that it is good or even natural to be a Native American. Native Americans tend to lag behind other groups in health services, fall between the cracks for government services, are getting decreasing aid for education, and often find it difficult to even prove that they are Native American in order to get what services exist. As of 1986 Los Angeles County had only one social worker for the entire Native American population, and only $200,000 budgeted for the whole community. It is assumed by government agencies that Native Americans will get all of their services on the reservation and therefore little provision is made for the urban dwellers. In addition they have been discriminated against; for example, authorities on occasion have denied Native Americans the right to practice their traditional religions. In one instance a fire department truck arrived to extinguish a sacred fire.

These problems were addressed at "Summit '88," a national conference for Native Americans sponsored by the Alliance of Native Americans, a Los Angeles group that was formed in March 1988, and held at California State University, Northridge. About 300 participants from 20 groups attended this first meeting. The conference planned to "address the political, economic and social issues facing American Indians." The delegates discussed lobbying politicians on Native American issues and called for more funds to aid the homeless and to establish a cultural center in Los Angeles. The conference was a milestone in generating cooperation among many different Native Amercian groups who traditionally have been so concerned with their differences that little common ground could be realized.

With their recent history filled with dissent, it is not surprising that most of the Native American culture in Los Angeles deals with past heritage rather than present accomplishments. Most current community attempts have only partial success—radio programs are scheduled at inconvenient times and *The Talking Leaf*, a one-time newspaper, is no longer published for lack of funds. On the other hand six Native American churches are to be found in the city, there are Native American Study Centers at five universities (California State University [CSU] Fullerton, CSU Long Beach, CSU Los Angeles, CSU Northridge, and UCLA) and there are four Native American Libraries. The most prominent monument to Native American artists of the past and present is the Southwest Museum, which houses a major collection of traditional Native American art and also exhibits contemporary Native American work. The Museum sponsors a Native American Film Festival every January, with films by or about Native Americans. In Southern California there are two pageants dedicated to "traditional" romantic Native American "happenings": the pageant of Ramona has been presented at Hemet since 1923, and The Cross and the Arrow, a pageant of *La Christianita* at San Clemente, depicts that area's place in California history.

A number of powwows (meetings of Native Americans) are held in the Los Angeles area every year, including one at UCLA in April sponsored by the UCLA American Indian Center, one in Orange County in July sponsored by the Southern California Indian Center, and an Annual American Indian Festival at the Natural History Museum in December, featuring demonstrations, lectures and exhibits. At the three-day intertribal powwow at the Santa Monica Civic Auditorium in June 1988, more than 100 Native Americans from all over the United States and Canada participated in traditional dances and rituals. "A powwow is both a social gathering and a glorification of the warrior," noted Glenda Ahhaitty, one of the powwow coordinators. War dances today honor those who serve in the contemporary military.

■ Black (African American)

In 1786, Maria Rita Valdez, whose Black grandparents were among the founders of Los Angeles, owned a 4,500 acre ranch called Rodeo de las Aguas *(Meeting of Waters). Today this area is known as Beverly Hills. Francisco Reyes, who was part Black, sold the San Fernando Valley in the 1790s and became mayor of Los Angeles.*

The Black population of Los Angeles was extremely small until the twentieth century, despite the fact that the history of African Americans in the city goes back to the founding settlers—of the 22 adults who originally came from Mexico, ten were Black. The 1850 census recorded a dozen African Americans, only one of whom (Peter Biggs, also known as "Pedro") was given a surname; this may have been because Biggs, a barber, was one of the few Blacks who was self-employed rather than a servant in a White household. In 1880 there were a mere 188 Blacks in all of Los Angeles County, most living in what is today Little Tokyo. By 1920 there were about 19,000, which was still less than three percent of the population.

The years between 1900 and 1929 are often referred to as the Golden Era for Blacks in Los Angeles; the term does not imply that that there was no discrimination but rather that they were able to live better— many were able to buy homes—than in the places in which they had been born. The Los Angeles Forum, founded in 1903, was a "club of intelligent colored men from the various churches of the city" whose purpose, according to newspaper accounts of the time, was to encourage "united effort on the part of Negroes for their advance and to strengthen them along lines of moral, social, intellectual, financial and Christian ethics." The group gave the Black community a sense of unity and pride, urged businesses to hire Blacks in other than menial positions, and mainly provided a forum for public debate and the airing of grievances. In 1910 36 percent of Black Angelenos, in various areas of the city, owned their own homes (as opposed to about two and a half percent in New York and 11 percent in New Orleans). The 1920s and 1930s saw the development of the Central-Adams area called "Sugar Hill," which was home to the successful Black community including entertainers Hattie McDaniel and Ethel Waters. (The Santa Monica Freeway cut the area in half when it was built in the 1960s.) At the same time Abbot Kinney, the founder of Venice, employed Blacks for the Kinney Amusement Company and a small African American community was established in Venice. One member, Arthur Reese, decorated the Venice Dance Pavilion as an indoor garden and "designed the huge revolving ball with bits of mirror on its surface, the kind of ball you see in movies of the period, with colored spotlights turning the ball into a magical predecessor of rock-n'-roll high-tech light shows."

By the end of the 1920s this era of peace and prosperity was fading; discrimination and racial problems were on the rise, stoked in part by the reemergence of the Ku Klux Klan as a reaction to the movie *Birth of a Nation*. During the 1920s and 1930s when the Black population was increasing, housing restrictions began to be applied and the Black population was forced into south-central Los Angeles. (Previous housing restrictions had been applied to Jews and Japanese.) This discrimination fostered businesses such as the Golden State Mutual Life Insurance Company, which began in 1925 to provide insurance, no longer available from White-owned companies, to Blacks. By 1940 Golden State was the largest Black-owned company in the West. The African American population remained concentrated for many years; in 1940 98 percent lived in the city proper. In 1943, when the Japanese were evacuated, Blacks moved into Little Tokyo.

The Black population increased with the aircraft industry boom of the 1940s and the resultant scarcity of manpower. Blacks were now deemed employable and thousands of them, mainly from rural towns in the South, where economic changes had been disastrous for agriculture, poured into Los Angeles. This influx nearly tripled the number of Blacks in the County—by 1950 there were 218,000—and sent older Blacks west and south of south-central Los Angeles.

The population continued to increase after the war and Blacks began to gain political recognition partly as a result of economic advances made during the war. Los Angeles was one of the first large cities to vote Blacks into office; Tom Bradley, Gilbert Lindsay and others became members of the City Council in the 1950s and 1960s. State government tried to alleviate racial discrimination. In 1958 Governor Pat Brown created the California Fair Employment Practices Commission, and in 1963 the Rumford Act, which prohibited racial discrimination in housing by landlords and real-estate agents, was passed by the California legislature.

The Rumford Act was ironically the indirect cause of what came to be known as the Watts Riots; in 1964 the Act was repealed by a substantial vote (it was particularly unattractive to those Whites living near Black sections of the city) and the African-American community, already angered over what they saw as other anti-Black incidents, rioted in August of 1965. Clark describes the consequences:

> Over . . . six days black and white-owned businesses were burned out over an area of 11 square miles, causing property damage of over $40 million. Thirty-four were killed in the riots; 28 of them black. A thousand were wounded or injured. Nearly 4,000 people were arrested. By the end of the week, South Central Los Angeles was held by an occupying force of 22,500 city and county police and 13,900 guardsmen.

The area never recovered from this disaster, and real or perceived discrimination of Blacks in the city continues to surface. Recently, nearly 25 years after the riots, an eight-square-mile area encompassing Watts, Willowbrook and Florence was finally slated for redevelopment by 1991.

Today there are large numbers of Black Americans in Los Angeles County—probably well over 950,000—but Blacks are vacating the city in increasing numbers. Between 73,000 and 76,000 left between 1975 and 1980, most it is believed because of the high cost of housing. Predictions are that by 1990 more African Americans will be leaving the metropolitan area than will be moving in; about half relocate in other parts of California, the rest move to other states.

The majority of Blacks have been and continue to be poor; many were originally drawn to Watts because the land was inexpensive and considered undesirable by the White community. When the African-American population became so substantial that Whites feared that a "Black" town with a Black mayor would emerge, Watts was annexed. Watts Towers has become the symbol of the Los Angeles Black community, the focus of the Black Art Center and the home of the Annual Simon Rodia Watts Towers Music and Arts Festival.

Los Angeles' Black community today, however, has in many ways moved out of the ghetto. There has been a Black mayor, Tom Bradley, for fifteen years and Black members of the City Council for over thirty. Several areas of the city in addition to Watts (which is 86 percent Black), are predominantly Black. In 1980 the city of Inglewood was 55 percent African American, had a Black mayor and the highest individual income and educational level for Blacks in any large city in the United States. View Park in Baldwin Hills is described by the Los Angeles *Times* as "one of the relatively few neighborhoods in the United States that is both solidly Black and solidly upper-middle class," since most Blacks moving ahead economically seek to live in White neighborhoods.

Black institutions in the city include the Black American Cinema Society of the Western States Black Research Center, the Aquarian Bookstore, the Brockman Gallery, the California Afro-American Museum and the Ebony Showcase Theatre. The Dunbar Hotel (previously the Somerville Hotel) in south-central Los Angeles, a hub of Black culture in the 1930s, 1940s and 1950s—and the only place in Los Angeles where visiting Blacks could stay (a West Coast Cross between the Cotton Club and the Waldorf-Astoria)—has received a multi-million dollar renovation. The Dunbar is now both a museum for Black entertainment memorabilia and a hotel for low-income housing; the income from the hotel allows the Museum to be self-supporting. St. Brigid Catholic Church in south-central Los Angeles has a liturgy imbued with Black cultural sensibilities. The Afro-American Resource Center "provides reference and referral services for libraries and the general public. Emphasis is placed on social, historical, and cultural information by and about Black Americans."

A Black newspaper, *The California Eagle* (originally called *The Advocate*), was founded as early as 1891 as a source of information and an advocate of justice. A second journal, *The Liberator*, joined the crusade for Black rights around the turn of the century—"Devoted to the cause of good government and the advance of the Afro-American," read the masthead. Current Black newspapers are the *Los Angeles Sentinel* (founded in 1933), which has aided the Black community in voicing their opinions and fighting discrimination, and *The Wave Newspapers*, begun as a chain of weeklies in the 1960s. A pioneering Black journalist was Los Angeles' Fay M. Jackson, who, in the late 1920s, founded the first Black news magazine on the West Coast. *Flash*, published in 1928 and 1929, featured articles by Jackson about the inequities faced by Blacks, including the poor wages earned by Black actors. In the 1930s Jackson helped found a Black women's magazine dedicated to helping women find jobs, and also became the first Black Hollywood correspondent for the Associated Negro Press. Her ventures were all short-lived, as financing proved difficult.

The second annual Black family reunion was held in Exposition Park in August of 1988. The program, sponsored by the National Council of Negro Women and other groups, was started "as a response to growing concern about the disintegration of the Black family." Celebrating "the history, tradition and culture of the Black family" the reunions attempt to combat negative images of Blacks by focusing on the positive aspects of the community. The event offers art, music and food as well as 26 pavilions with changing hourly programs about family values, health and fitness, young adult groups, senior citizen and handicapped needs, and general information.

There is also in Los Angeles a small Black immigrant population from Belize and the West Indies, probably between 50,000 and 100,000 people. The Jamaicans are the largest group followed by Haitians and Trinidadians. An annual Caribbean Carnival, organized by the local galleries, is held in south-central Los Angeles around Mardi Gras, with a parade from Rodeo and Crenshaw to Menlo Park. Haitians, Cubans, Trinidadians and some Nigerians participate; in 1988 about 10,000 people attended.

The Garifuna (Garinagu as they call themselves) are known as Black Caribs, the descendents of escaped African slaves who intermarried with the Arawak Indians about 300 years ago on the island of St. Vincent and who later moved to the Honduran Coast. There are 3,000 to 5,000 in Los Angeles today. Garifuna Settlement Day, celebrating the first Garifuna settlement in Belize in 1823, is held in mid-November at an Inglewood Church. Mass is followed by day-long singing, dancing and drumming as well as the crowning of the Settlement Day Queen. There is then an evening dance.

The "Belize-Caribbean pulse" and a Jamaican program can be heard on radio station KPFK.

Watts Towers, Watts

*Foreign-language Newspapers published
in Los Angeles County*

Los Angeles Tomorrow

At the dawning of the twenty-first century, Los Angeles will continue to be home to more races, religions, cultures, languages and peoples than any other city in the world. Despite the slow growth advocated by an increasing number of residents and politicians, the city is expected to grow at the rate of 2.1 percent a year, more than twice the national rate. Los Angeles, in fact, is the only big city in the industrial world that is still growing rapidly. If present trends continue, by the year 2000, the population of Southern California will be over 18 million and the overflow from Los Angeles will continue to spill into Orange, Ventura, San Bernardino and Riverside Counties.

Immigration is expected to decline over the next 20 years with population growth coming mainly from natural increases within the resident population. Most sources agree that the Hispanic and Asian populations will continue to mushroom and, if current trends continue (as noted in a 1989 Department of Health Services Report), by the year 2000 they will likely comprise over 56 percent (39 percent Hispanic and 17 percent Asian) of the county population (the city and the LAUSD will have an even higher percentage of Hispanics). The remaining 44 percent will be 33 percent White and 11 percent Black.

As Americans, particularly White Americans, continue to live longer, California and Los Angeles will increasingly house the elderly and minorities. This will mean that the working-age population—mainly Hispanics but also Blacks and Asians—will be asked to support the aging Anglos. White males in the work force are expected to decrease from the current 45 to 50 percent to about 25 percent by the year 2000. Service providers will be more and more concerned with multi-lingual and multi-cultural issues. If these projections are correct, California and Los Angeles are once again in the forefront of changing immigration and ethnic patterns, and Los Angeles may be the first large city to have its Anglo population dependent on minorities.

Despite the fact that the economy will expand, there is some concern that many Hispanics and Blacks will not benefit since the jobs created will largely be managerial and technical, and it is expected that people of color will continue to be underrepresented in these areas. Minority occupational distribution has not altered since 1975, and probably will not, unless there are significant changes in education and economic development. This means that African Americans and Hispanics will continue to cluster in slow-growing technology areas and machinery manufacturing; that is, relatively unskilled jobs which reap low wages. If this proves to be true, there is cause for concern that the economy may falter as the population becomes proportionally less well trained and educated. Similarly, support for the elderly may increasingly divert resources earmarked for education, social services and maintenance of public facilities such as streets and sewers.

The most difficult questions for the future are those concerning the effects of a multiracial society and the extent of acculturation. No group remains static, and interracial marriages are increasing. In some populations, more people marry outside of their ethnic group than within it; the Japanese, for example, have a 60 percent rate of intermarriage. A new multiracial population is rapidly emerging; there are children in Los Angeles who have a Black, Hispanic, White and Asian grandparent. There are few statistics on the multiracial population because, at present, everyone is counted as a member of one of only four racial groups—Asian, Black, Hispanic or White. It is not predictable whether the merging of certain economic and social groups will increase as a result of greater numbers of multiracial individuals.

In a November 1988 article in the Los Angeles *Times*, Itaberi Njeri suggests that Los Angeles as the imagined perfect melting pot does not yet exist. There are alleged cases of discrimination by minorities against those of mixed race and of minorities against minorities. One response to the increasing multiracial population has been the founding of MASC, Multiracial Americans of Southern California, "a cultural and educational support group for racially and culturally mixed families and those interested in promoting multicultural understanding," which held its second annual conference in 1988.

Most immigrant groups have a deeply ingrained pride in maintaining their cultural identity, and the continuation of many local traditions has caused people to describe Los Angeles as a stew or salad rather than a melting pot. In general, studies of ethnicity have found that first-generation immigrants are more concerned with survival and having their children assimilate than they are with tradition, that the second generation delights in being American and that the third, secure in their Americanness, becomes interested in rediscovering their roots. As we have seen, however, some ethnic groups acculturate more readily than others and there are no hard and fast rules. Whatever the extent of acculturation, we can safely predict that its effects promise to influence many facets of city life, from politics to business to the arts. The fate of ethnic institutions such as banks and driving schools will to some degree depend on the group being served and how important assimilation is for that particular community. It is likely that Asians will continue to assimilate to "American" life faster than Hispanics, although Los Angeles increasingly will become a Hispanic city.

The extent to which ethnic communities, particularly the large Hispanic ones, find their political voices will also have an impact on the changing face of the area. Minorities in general and the Hispanics in particular are becoming more vocal and agitated about their place—or lack of it—in politics and community organizations. As today's young Hispanic community comes of age, it may be presumed that more will use their franchise to vote and demand the representation that Hispanics should have, based on their numbers. The Asian populations too are moving away from their traditional political apathy and becoming more active in community affairs.

The areas of the city occupied by ethnic groups will continue to change as they always have, but predicting how and when is more difficult. Asians, particularly in Monterey Park and surrounding areas in the San Gabriel Valley, appear to be becoming more concentrated geographically, while the Hispanic population seems to be dispersing. Pockets that emerge when large numbers of people arrive at the same time— such as the Armenians in Hollywood—will no doubt fan out as future generations become comfortable with English and with American society, as such communities have in the past.

As the population of the Southern California megalopolis increases and the Los Angeles area continues to incorporate sections of the surrounding counties, young people of any background may find these adjoining counties to be the only places where they can afford to live. This shift may affect low-income ethnic groups in that if jobs are concentrated in the city, they will have longer distances to travel in order to get to work.

If tomorrow's ethnic Los Angeles retains some elements of today's we should continue to see the appearance of the likes of the Hsi Lai and Sree Venkateswara Temples, be able to participate in ethnic ceremonies such as The Blessing of the Animals and shop at places like the African Marketplace. These are, and will be, among the joys of Los Angeles.

Japanese Drummers, Los Angeles

Celebrations

A partial listing of ethnic religious days, celebrations and get-togethers held in the Los Angeles area.

■ January

Early	NATIVE AMERICAN Film Festival Southwest Museum
1st Sunday	JAPANESE New Year, Oshogatsu Japanese American Cultural and Community Center
Sunday after January 6	GREEK ORTHODOX Blessing of the Water Queen Mary, Long Beach

■ February

Early	CHINESE New Year Chinatown
2nd Saturday	MAYA Fiesta of Santa Eulalia Varying locations

■ March

	CARIBBEAN Carnival South Central Los Angeles
Mid	JEWISH Arts Festival Claremont McKenna College

17	IRISH St. Patrick's Day Parade Hollywood
25	GREEK Feast of Annunciation Saint Sophia Greek Orthodox Cathedral
Palm Sunday	UKRAINIAN Pysanky and Ritual Bread Exhibition Ukrainian Cultural Center
Day before Easter	MEXICAN Blessing of the Animals Olvera Street

■ April

Mid	NATIVE AMERICAN Powwow UCLA, Ackerman Union
Mid	THAI New Year Wat Thai Temple
Mid	CAMBODIAN New Year
Late	SCOTS Fiddlers of Los Angeles Contest John Adams Jr. High School, Santa Monica
Late	MIDDLE EASTERN Eid-Ul-Fitr Islamic Celebration New Horizon School, South Pasadena
Late	JEWISH Festival Rancho Park, West Los Angeles

■ May

ISRAELI Independence Day Walk Festival
Rancho Park

LATIN Carnaval
Long Beach

Saturday before May 5	MEXICAN Cinco de Mayo Roosevelt and Lennox Parks (Parade starts at USC)
Early	ASIAN PACIFIC American Heritage Week Various Locations
Early	AFRICAN Heritage Festival
Early	PORTUGUESE Lady of Fatima Celebration Artesia
Early	POLYNESIAN Dance Festival Laguna Hills
1st Sunday	JAPANESE Children's Day Little Tokyo
Mid	PHILIPPINE Heritage Festival and Santa Cruz de Mayo Philippine Town
17	NORWEGIAN Constitution Day San Pedro
Memorial Day Weekend	AFRICA Liberation Day Weekend Various Locations

■ June

2nd weekend	IRISH Fair and Music Festival Burbank
2nd weekend	MEXICAN Feria de los Niños Hollenbeck Park
28	PERUVIAN Independence Day Peruvian Consulate

CELEBRATIONS

■ July

1	CANADIAN Dominion Day Several locations
2nd Sunday	CROATIAN Festival Alpine Village
Mid	FRENCH Bastille Day Triforium
Mid	HAWAIIAN Ho'olaule'a Alondra Park, Lawndale
3rd weekend	ASIAN/PACIFIC ISLANDER Day of the Lotus Festival Echo Park Lake
3rd weekend July, Aug., Sept.	AFRICAN Marketplace James H. Whitworth Park
Late	AFRICAN AMERICAN Simon Rodia Watts Towers Music and Art Festival Watts Towers Art Center
Late	PORTUGUESE Holy Ghost Celebration Artesia
Last weekend	NATIVE AMERICAN Powwow Costa Mesa

■ August

	JAPANESE Oban Festival West Los Angeles Buddhist Temple (and other Temples)
Mid	JAPANESE Nisei Week Little Tokyo
Mid	INDIA Independence Day Various Locations

Late	JEWISH Yiddish Culture Festival Plummer Park
Late	AFRICAN-AMERICAN Family Reunion Exposition Park
Late	SAMOAN Flag Day Carson

■ September

	AFRICAN Drum Festival
	GREEK Festival Santa Anita Race Track, Arcadia
	JAPANESE Cultural Show Gardena
	PACIFIC ISLANDER Festival Harbor Regional Park
Labor Day Weekend	AFRICAN-AMERICAN Mahalia Jackson Gospel Music Festival California State University, Los Angeles
Labor Day Weekend	GREEK Festival by the Sea Long Beach
Mid	MEXICAN Independence Day West Los Angeles
Mid	KOREAN Festival Koreatown
3rd Sunday	BELIZEAN Day in the Park Jackie Robinson Stadium
Last Saturday	GUATEMALAN San Miguel Festival Various Locations
Late	CAMBODIAN Festival of Ancestors, *Pchum Ben*

CELEBRATIONS

■ October

GERMAN Oktoberfest
Various locations

Early   GREEK St. Katherine Festival
Torrance

Early   ARMENIAN Cultural Festival
Various locations

1st weekend ASANTE Cultural Day
Culver City Veteran's Auditorium

1st weekend LITHUANIAN Fair
St. Casmir's Church

1st weekend SCOTS Pacific Highland Gatherings and Games
Chino Fairgrounds (Pomona)

3rd weekend SERBIAN Anniversary of St. Sava Church
St. Sava Serbian Orthodox Church

Late   CELTIC Samhain Fleadh Ceol-Celtic New Year
Celtic Arts Center

■ November

1st weekend MEXICAN Day of the Dead
Several Locations

Early   JEWISH Festival of Artisans
Temple Isaiah

Mid   GARIFUNA Settlement Day Celebration
St. Francis X. Cabrini Church

Late   SAMOAN Culture Day
Polynesian Island Village, Laguna Hills

◼ December

1st Sunday	UKRAINIAN Open House and Exhibition Ukrainian Art Center
1st weekend	NATIVE AMERICAN Festival Natural History Museum
13	SWEDISH Lucia Day
Mid	MEXICAN Los Posadas Olvera Street and other locations
Late	AFRICAN Kwanza Festival Various locations

Sree Venkateswara Temple (detail),
Calabasas

Religious Monuments

The following is a list of some of the larger religious structures referred to in the text; most have been built in traditional styles following traditional precedents.

These monuments announce the establishment of an immigrant community. They are an indication that the group has put down roots and has the capabilities to raise the money and manpower necessary to produce substantial religious structures. These buildings hail both the origins of a people and their coming-of-age in a new land.

HIGASHI HONGANJI
Buddhist (Japanese)
505 East 3rd Street
Little Tokyo

HOLY VIRGIN MARY CATHEDRAL
Russian Orthodox
650 Michel Torena
Silver Lake

HSI LAI TEMPLE
Buddhist (Chinese)
3456 Glenmark Drive
Hacienda Heights, East San Gabriel Valley

KHEMARA BUDDIKARAM
Buddhist (Cambodian)
1056 Cherry Avenue
Long Beach

MATKA BOSKA CZESTOCHOWA
Polish
3424 West Adams Boulevard
Los Angeles

NORWEGIAN SEAMAN'S CHURCH
1035 South Beacon Street
San Pedro

OUR LADY QUEEN OF ANGELS
535 North Main Street
Los Angeles

ST. CASIMIR
Lithuanian
2718 St. George St.
Los Angeles

ST. SOPHIA
Greek Orthodox
1324 South Normandie
Los Angeles

SREE VENKATESWARA TEMPLE
Hindu
1600 Las Virgenes Canyon Road
Calabasas

WAT THAI
Buddhist (Thai)
8225 Coldwater Canyon Rd.
North Hollywood

RELIGIOUS MONUMENTS

Newspapers

The number of ethnic- and immigrant-oriented newspapers both in English and "foreign" languages, which are published in the Los Angeles area, has increased dramatically in the past two decades. The following is a partial list of these newspapers and the communities they service. When the information is available, the frequency of publication and founding date have been noted.

Arab

News Circle, monthly magazine

Armenian

Armenian Observer
California Courier
Yerkoonk, monthly

Asian

Asiam, monthly magazine for upscale Asian Americans

Black

Central News Wave, weekly, founded 1919
Eagle Rock Sentinel, bi-weekly, founded 1910
Firestone Park News/Southern News Press, weekly, founded 1924
The *Sentinel*, weekly, founded 1933
Watts Star Review, weekly, founded 1975
The *Wave Newspapers*, a chain of weeklies founded in the 1960s

Chinese

Centre Daily News, daily (ceased publication September 1989)
Chinese Times
Indo-Chinese News
International Daily News, daily, founded 1981
New Kwong Tat Press
Pacific Journal

Sing Tao Newspapers
Southern California Chinese News
T'ai Chi, Chinese discipline and meditiation, founded 1977
Tai Wan Tribune
Tribune Chinese Newspapers
United Times
Vietnam-Chinese Newspapers
World Daily News, daily
Young China Daily

Dutch
Holland News

Filipino
California Examiner, weekly, founded 1983
Los Angeles Philippine News, weekly
Philippine American News, bi-monthly

German
California Staats-Zeitung, weekly, founded 1890

Hungarian
California Magyarsag (California Hungarians), weekly, founded 1922

Irish
Irish American Press, monthly

Israeli
Hadshot L.A., weekly
Israel Shelanu, weekly

Japanese
Gateway USA, biweekly
Kashu Mainichi, daily, founded 1931
Pacific Citizen, weekly, founded 1929
Rafu Shimpo, daily
Tozai Times

Jewish
B'nai Brith Messenger, weekly, founded 1917
Heritage, weekly, founded 1954
Israel Today, bimonthly
Jewish Community Bulletin

Korean

Dong-A I/Bo, daily
Korea Times, daily
Korean Central Daily, daily
Korean Culture, daily, founded 1980
The *New Korea*, weekly

Lithuanian

Lietuviu Dienos (*Lithuanian Days*), monthly, founded 1946

Persian (Farsi)

Rah-e-Zendigi, monthly

Polish

Panorama of Polonia

Russian

Panorama, weekly

Spanish

Belvedere Citizen, weekly, founded 1934
Brooklyn-Belvedere Comet, weekly, founded 1950
City Terrace Comet, weekly, founded 1950
Eastside Sun, weekly, founded 1945
El Diario daily, founded 1987
El Serano Star, weekly, founded 1949
La Opinion, daily, founded 1926
La Vox Libre (Cuban)
La Vox Libre, weekly magazine, founded 1981
Low Rider, monthly, geared to Chicano lifestyle, founded 1972
Mexican-American Sun, weekly, founded 1950
Montebello Comet, weekly, founded 1974
Monterey Park Comet, weekly, founded 1974
Mr. Teve, entertainment weekly
Noticias del Mundo, daily, founded 1984
20 de Mayo (Cuban)
Wyvernwood Chronicle, weekly, founded 1950

Thai

Sereechai, weekly

Vietnamese

Thoi Luan

Restaurant Signs

Restaurants and Markets

For many people the ethnicity of a city is measured by what they can eat. By this standard alone Los Angeles may be the most ethnically diverse city in the country; food and ingredients from almost anywhere in the world are available in restaurants, to take out, or in markets.

Restaurants cater to different segments of the population. Those well known to many Angelenos and visitors, and found all over the metropolitan area, include Mexican eateries serving burritos, tamales and mole; Chinese dishing out chop suey and chow mein; Japanese offering teriyaki and sushi (which ten years ago Angelenos considered anathema), and Indian fare such as samosas and curries. Thai restaurants, in recent years, have become almost as numerous as Mexican, and French, Italian, Greek and Korean are almost as easy to find as a hamburger joint.

Fewer people might know that there are vegetarian Indian eateries, Mexican restaurants that specialize in seafood (mariscos) or foods of a particular region (Yucatan, Jalisco), Chinese that offer up Mongolian barbecue, and Japanese that serve only noodles (ramen) or specialize in eel dishes.

With a little additional research one can discover the delights of eating Cuban (pork and plantains), Jamaican (curried goat and ackee), British (fish and chips), Hungarian (cold cherry soup and goulash), Yugoslavian (roast lamb shanks and dumplings), German (roast goose and sausage), Kosher Deli (pastrami and kreplach), Ethiopian (steak tartare with injera), Persian (kebabs and raw garlic in vinegar), and Indonesian (gado-gado and chicken in coconut milk).

Less common but also catering to the metropolitan population are restaurants specializing in the foods of Argentina, Brazil, Morocco, Afghanistan, Russia, Poland and West Africa. There are also the "mixed" restaurants—Argentinian/Italian, Peruvian/Chinese, Irish/Indian, Mexican/Indian and French/Mexican. One Venice "New York-style" delicatessen will deliver quesadilla or nachos as well as pastrami sandwiches.

Truly serious ethnic eaters can find—but generally only in the neighborhoods housing the population and where the visitors are likely to be the only "foreigners" in the place—Guatemalan, Nicaraguan, Salvadoran, Bolivian, Chilean, Colombian, Ecuadorean, Peruvian, Czechoslovakian and Romanian restaurants. For any immigrant group, but particularly those newly arrived or here in small numbers, a place which serves "home" cooking and where one can find people speaking a familiar language or dialect fulfills important social and psychological needs as well as hunger pangs.

Some ethnic foods have by now joined the mainstream of Los Angeles' culinary offerings. As in other metropolitan areas pasta and pizza are not considered foreign foods and Angelenos are as likely to have a taco or a burrito (or even a kosher burrito) for lunch as a hamburger or tuna fish sandwich. Tostada bowls and Chinese chicken salad appear as standard fare on coffee shop menus. Chains, like Mrs. Garcia's and El Pollo Loco, are not owned or necessarily run by those of Mexican descent. Some "ethnic" foods—such as tortillas and water chestnuts—can be found in most area supermarkets; more recently sushi has begun to appear in many. Almost all supermarkets have an ethnic food section and many these days cater to the needs of the ethnic group (or groups) in the neighborhood, with large portions of the store devoted to Mexican, Armenian or Chinese meats, fish, produce and spices. In some of these markets, and in the more specialized stores, one can find more specialized items—food and accoutrements for almost any cuisine.

In *Cook's Marketplace Los Angeles*, Burum and Virbila tell us that the following and much more is available in Los Angeles area markets:

Jamaican
Yellow yams (resembling a scaly elephant's foot)

Costa Rican
Coconuts and cassava

African
Dried shrimp, red palm oil, dried salt cod, plantain chips, cleaned and boxed conch meat

Chinese

Chicken feet, hog maws, cleaned squid, cured stripped pork, duck feet, pork snout and ears, honeycomb tripe, wheat gluten puffs, rice-flour dumplings, frozen bao, scallion cakes, shao bing (sesame buns stuffed with minced pork and onions), Mandarin orange peel, alum crystals, lemon grass powder, taro root flour, and oyster and hoisin sauce sold by weight

Malay

Curry spices

Dutch

Roggereye, smoked sprats, stollen, "Bacon" cake (when sliced the dark and light layers look like bacon), boeren kas (gouda cheese made from unpastcurized milk), herring, speculaas (honey gingerbread available at Christmas)

Indonesian

Krupuk (shrimp chips), boemkoe (spice mixture), chile-shrimp paste, bogor nuts, ketjap (sticky soy sauce), creamed coconut

Russian

Caviar, smoked koppchyunka (tiny fish)

Hungarian

Hazelnut torte, blood sausage, fustolt szalona (aged smoked bacon), paprika peppers, paprika bacon, smoked goose breast, sweetened chestnut puree, head cheese and potato bread

Bulgarian

Yogurt

Yugoslavian

Angel-hair pasta, sardines, fruit nectars, bocconcini (small mozzarella-like cheeses made without preservatives)

Philippine

Tocino (marinated pork belly), longaniza (sausage with vinegar, garlic and a little brown sugar), "tofu pudding," fresh soybean juice, hopia mongo (pork fat pastries stuffed with mung beans), patola (a cucumber-like vegetable), panucha (unrefined sugar wrapped in leaves), upo (gourd), yam jam, whole bangus fish, hot banana ketchup, sugar cane vinegar and cans of bagoongs

German

Sausage, breads, butter, salz herring in brine, apfel korn (apple schnaps), dried mushrooms from the Black Forest, more than 50 kinds of *Viennese* sausage

Czech

Plum brandy

Polish

Kielbasa

Hawaiian

Pickled Maui onions, sweet bread, poi, and laulau (pork and butterfish mixed with taro leaves, wrapped in ti leaves and steamed)

Indian

Basmati rice, chick pea flour, brown-bean flour, fresh chapatis, spice pastes for curry, dal, pappadams

Italian

Sausage, cheeses, fresh pasta, panettone at Christmas, calves liver, fresh or frozen baby goats, fresh made tomato puree, cannoli, sfogliatelle.

Japanese

Zuke (pickles), dried seaweed, soba noodles, sushi-makings, natto (fermented soy beans), low-sodium miso, bread, fresh matsutake mushrooms, gobo, daikon, yaki karei (broiled seasoned whitefish or flounder), senbe, kabocha (pumpkins), and gyoza (dumpling) filling

Korean

Radish, sesame leaf, radish and cabbage kim chee, cuttlefish, soobac (soy sauce), hot chile oil, dangmyun noodles, and beef tripe

Argentinian

Cotijo cheese, guava paste, sour cream based bread, prepared yuca, flan

Brazilian

Marrons glacés

Colombian
Potatoes (papas criollas)

Peruvian
Dried potatoes

Spanish
Capers, white asparagus and roasted sweet red peppers

Mexican
Queso ranchero, quince paste, many kinds of dried chiles, gasper goo (fish), fried milk (a sweet) and manzanilla seeds

Cuban
Diced beef

Greek
filo dough, homemade yogurt, wild onions in brine and butter cookies

Armenian
Pizza and honey

Egyptian
Dried black mullet roe

Syrian
Saffron

Swedish
Sprats, crayfish in dill sauce and limpa

Norwegian
Mustard, cod, and goat cheese

Finnish
Blue cheese

Danish
Rye and syrups

New Zealand
Eel

Thai

Sweet chile sauce, yellow bean sauce, tea, dried kafir, and powdered galangal (related to ginger), sambals

Vietnamese

Fish balls, pâtés and sausages.

One can also get bagels, Chinese cookware, cookbooks for many kinds of cuisine, jars of Asian dried roots and herbs, ginseng in many varieties, dried sea horses, swallow's nests (for bird's nest soup), seeds to grow your own Chinese leeks and bok choy, spaetzle makers, German back oblaten (edible cookie sheet liner that doesn't have to be peeled off), Indian toothpaste, sweetbreads, brains, fresh cow's feet, suckling pigs, dried hibiscus flowers, fresh watermelon juice, eggplant relish with mint and garlic, dried lime, coconut milk, pot stickers, gai lin (white flowered broccoli), dried shark's fin, black mushrooms, sea cucumbers, almond powder, rice flour, fresh lily root stems, lemon grass, live turtles, eels and catfish, fresh lotus root, Chinese chive flowers, fung sang ("sea blubber"), salted jellyfish, pancakes for mu shu pork and fresh water chestnuts. There is wine from Hungary, Yugoslavia, Germany, Greece, the Balkans, Chile, Argentina, Australia and Cyprus.

Foods available to take out include Indonesian lumpia, martabak (beef "omelette"), gado-gado salad and bami-goreng (fried noodles); Italian cannelloni, lasagne and marinara sauce; Argentinian empanadas; Mexican carnitas and menudo; Middle Eastern borek and kefti; and Thai roasted peanuts with coconut. Indian and Japanese fast food take-outs have joined Middle Eastern felafal sandwiches (on pita) and Mexican tacos.

Recommending specific restaurants or stores is difficult since many of these come and go—some before you even find them—but I refer you, for the present to:

Linda Burum and S. Irene Virbila *Cook's Marketplace Los Angeles*. San Francisco: 101 Productions, 1986.

Shindler, Merrill. *Best Restaurants of Los Angeles under $10*. San Francisco: 101 Productions, 1989.

Restaurant Signs

Bibliography

Authors of direct quotes are indicated by chapter before the bibliographic entries.

LAT Los Angeles *Times*

LAHE Los Angeles *Herald Examiner*

Foreword

Clifford, Frank. "Census Mired in Dispute Over Counting the Hidden." LAT 3/15/89, I:1.

LA 2000: A City for the Future. Los Angeles 2000 Committee. 1988.

Roderick, Kevin. "Deciding What Counts in the 90s." LAT 3/14/89, I:1.

Introduction

Page 20 Carey McWilliams, pp. 52–53.

Page 20 Ibid. p. 55

Page 21 Ibid. p. 142.

Page 22 Ronald C. Woolsley, p. 90

Page 22 John D. Weaver, p. 16

Page 22 McWilliams, p. 150

Page 23 Ibid. p. 159

Page 24 Weaver, p. 84

Page 24 McWilliams, p. 158

Auerbach, Susan. *Cityroots Festival: A Celebration of New Immigrant Traditions*. City of Los Angeles Cultural Affairs Department, 1987.

Dembart, Lee, "Long Population Boom in L.A. Ending, Experts Say." LAT 5/14/84, I:3.

Du Brow, Rick. "KSCI's the Voice from Home for Local Asians." LAHE 5/21/88, C1.

Hanson, Earl and Paul Beckett. *Los Angeles: Its People and its Homes*. Los Angeles: The Haynes Foundation, 1944.

Harvey, Steve. "Early Visiting Celebrities Found L.A. a Dreary Place." LAT 9/13/87.

Hill, Laurance L. *La Reina: Los Angeles in Three Centuries*. Los Angeles: Security Trust and Savings Bank, 1929.

Inta, Edith. "County No. 1 in U.S. after 6-year Boom." LAHE 8/31/87, A1.

Lederer, Lillian Charlotte. "A Study of Anglo-American Settlers in Los Angeles County Previous to the Admission of California to the Union." Thesis, University of Southern California, 1927.

Los Angeles East Magazine (Supplement to the Mexican American Sun Group) V8 #2, 9/80:6.

McCarthy, Kevin. "The Slow-Growing Orange: A Demographer's Look at Future Los Angeles." The Rand Paper Series, P-6974, 1984.

McCarthy, Kevin. *Wall Street Journal*, 1/15/85:33.

McGarry, T.W. "Indian Feud: Development Brings Out the War Paint." LAT 6/4/88, II:1.

McWilliams, Carey. *Southern California: An Island on the Land*. Salt Lake City: Peregrine Smith, 1983 (First published 1946).

Stern, Gail F., ed. *Freedom's Doors: Immigrant Ports of Entry to the United States*. Philadelphia: The Balch Institute, 1986.

The California Missions: A Pictorial History. Menlo Park, California: Lane Book Co. (A Sunset Book), 1971.

Turpin, Dick. "Population Pressure on Housing." LAT 7/26/87, VIII:1.

Weaver, John D. *El Pueblo Grande*. Los Angeles: The Ward Ritchie Press, 1973.

Willard, Charles Dwight. *The Herald's History of Los Angeles City*. Los Angeles: Kingsley, Baines and Neuner Co., 1901.

Woolsley, Ronald C. "Rites of Passage? Anglo and Mexican American Contrasts in a Time of Change: Los Angeles, 1860–1870." In *Southern California Quarterly*, Summer 1987 LXIX:2.

Los Angeles Today

Page 29   Thomas B. Rosenstiel

Page 29   Charles Recksieck

Page 31   Dan Goodgame

Page 31   Myrna Oliver

Alessi, Nicole. "International faire highlights various cultures." *UCLA Daily Bruin* 4/16/87:3.

Bucy, Erik P. "No Work Shortage for Translators, Interpreters." LAHE 7/30/89, B1.

Chavez, Stephanie. "Crowds Dip into Melting Pot at Multiethnic 'City Roots Festival.' " LAT 5/31/87, II:3.

Clayton, Janet. "Tenuous New Alliances Forged to Ease Korean-Black Tensions." LAT 7/20/87, II:1.

DIAL. "KCET Celebrates Cultural Diversity Month." 10/87:8.

DIAL. "Cultural Diversity Month Specials." 10/88:28.

Feldman, Paul. "Turkish to Tagalog—L.A. Courts Hear it All." LAT 5/5/85, I:1.

Gindick, Tia. "Ethnic Weddings Still Flaunt Their Roots." LAT 10/9/83, VII:1.

Gollner, Philipp. "Common Ground: 700 Campus Clubs Bring UCLA Students Together." LAT 1/24/88, IX:1.

Good, Mary (KCSI). Letter, 2/9/88.

Goodgame, Dan. "Citizens in All but Name". *Time* 7/8/85.

Gordon, Larry. "Eastern Colleges: Recruiters Offer West A Taste of Ivy." LAT 12/13/88, I:1.

Hayes-Bautista, David E. *The Burden of Support: Young Latinos in an Aging Society*. Stanford University Press, 1988.

Hernandez, Marita. "Tale of 2 Cultures." LAT 5/18/86, II:1.

Hernandez, Marita. "Immigrant Teens Find Little Refuge." LAT 1/25/89, I:1.

Johnson, Marilyn (Los Angeles Public Library). Telephone Interview, September 28, 1988.

Los Angeles Folk Arts, Summer 1987, 2:2.

McCarthy, Kevin F. "Immigration and California: Issues for the 1980s." Santa Monica: The Rand Corporation, P-6846, 1983.

McCarthy, Kevin F. and R. Burciaga Valdez. "California's Demographic Future." 1986. Santa Monica: The Rand Corporation, N-2481-NICHD.

Melinkoff, Ellen. "Cityroots Festival to Celebrate L.A.'s Cultural, Ethnic Diversity." LAT 5/30/87, V:1.

Moffet, Penelope. "Latin Carnival Atmosphere Fills Streets of Long Beach." LAT 5/21/88, V:1.

Njeri, Itabari. " A Sense of Identity." LAT 6/5/88, VI:1.

Oliver, Myrna. "Cultural Defense—A Legal Tactic." LAT 7/15/88, I:1.

Recksieck, Charles. "Folk Art and City Roots: LA's Immigrant Experience." Immigration Research Report. UCLA Institute for Social Science Research, 1987 2:2.

Reinhold, Robert. "Courts Seeking Translators for Alien Cases." *The New York Times*, 8/11/87:1.

Reinhold, Robert. "The New California Dream: Closing the Door." *The New York Times* 6/12/88, E5.

Reuben, Liz. "Ratio of Asians will rise Fastest." LAHE 9/13/89: A1.

Rosenstiel, Thomas B. "L.A. Papers Speak a New Language." LAT 11/9/87, I:1.

Russell, George. "Trying to Stem the Illegal Tide." *Time* 7/8/85.

Washington Post 12/13/87, A1; 12/14/87, A1; 12/15/87, A1; 12/16/87; A1; 12/17/87,A1; 12/18/87, A1.

Wong, May. "Professor Says Californians Should Be Looking to Future." *Daily Bruin* 5/17/88:13.

Public Schools

Page 35   Stephanie Chavez, LAT 5/26/88

Page 36   Stephen Braun, LAT 12/30/84

Anderluh, Deborah. "Hispanics will Push L.A. Enrollment to Peak." LAHE 3/13/87:A3.

Biederman, Patricia Ward. "School Board Debate Heats Up on Ratio of Minorities." LAT 11/3/87, CC II:1.

Braun, Stephan. "Hollywood High: Many are Strangers in a Strange Land." LAT 9/16/84, IX:1.

Braun, Stephan. "Americanization: Fitting In Has a Price." LAT 12/30/84, IX:1.

Braun, Stephen. "Coping with Change." LAT 4/21/85,IX:1.

Chavez, Stephanie. "The Next Step: Classes Will Prepare 171,000 for Permanent U.S. Status." LAT 5/10/88, II:1.

Chavez, Stephanie. "'Red-Eye' Citizenship Classes Attract Aliens'." LAT 5/26/88, I:1.

Connell, Rich. "Ruling Could Ease School's Multilingual Problems." LAT 2/16/89, I:1.

Ferrell, David. "Immigrant Students Catch on Fast to New School's Mysteries." LAT 9/15/88, II:1.

Goldman, Jay. "School Becomes Portal to American Dream for Aliens Given Amnesty." 9/22/88, W:14.

Haldane, David. "Melting Pot: L.B.Schools Work to Assimilate Pupils of Many Tongues." LAT 3/2/86, LB X:1.

Hubler, Shawn. "Foreign Customs, abuse laws can clash in schools." LAHE 11/1/87: A1.

Koh, Barbara. "Spelling Out the American Way." LAT 8/17/89, W:1.

La Guire, Lenny and Shawn Hubler. "Many minorities add up to major new cultural force." LAHE 5/6/88, A1.

Madrigal, Hector (LAUSD). Telephone Interview 7/21/89.

McCarthy, Kevin F. & R. Burciaga Valdez. "California's Demographic Future." Santa Monica: The Rand Corporation, N-2481-NICHD. 1986.

Mendosa, Rick. "How Long Can the Children Wait?" *Hispanic Business* 7/89:18B.

Milstein, Michael. "School District Gets Jump in Producing Amnesty Material." LAT 6/21/88, II:3.

Olsen, Laurie. *Crossing the Schoolhouse Border: Immigrant Students and the California Public Schools*. A California Tomorrow Policy Research Report, 1988.

Oswald, John A. "L.A. Eases Way for Immigrant Pupils." LAT 9/7/88, II:3.

Reid, Tish (LAUSD). Interview 9/29/87

Savage, David. G. "Hollywood High Gets a Global Cast." LAT 6/20/82 I:1

Wilcove, M.J. "Educating Rita, Rosita and Mi-Kyung: An Essay on Trusting the Children." *L.A. Weekly* 11/6–12/87:16.

Wilkinson, Tracy. "Class Action." LAT 3/6/88,IX:1.

Woo, Elaine. "The Changing Face of L.A.'s Schools." LAT 3/13/87:II:1.

Woo, Elaine. "Ethnic Diversity Puts School Districts to Test." LAT 4/9/87, SGV IX:1

Woo, Elaine. "Debate Continues to Rage Over Bilingual Education." LAT 2/10/88, I:1.

Woo, Elaine. "Mexico's Education Secretary Studies L.A. Bilingual Effort." LAT 3/5/88, II:3

Woo, Elaine. "New Plan Offered on Bilingual Education." LAT 3/18/88, II:9.

Woo, Elaine. "Immigrants Having Hard Time in U.S. Schools, Study Says." LAT 4/21/88, II:3.

Woo, Elaine. "$3.5 Billion OKd for L.A. Schools' 1988–89 Budget." LAT 8/23/88, II:1

Business

Page 39   Dick Turpin

Page 41   Linda Williams, LAT 5/28/88

Page 43   Ruth Ryon

Page 44   Carlos V. Lozano

Applegate, Jane. "Cutting Across Cultural Lines." LAT 12/12/88, IV:5.

Becklund, Laurie. "300 Latino Leaders at Conference Target Agenda of '90s." LAT 10/29/88, II:1.

Bradsher, Keith. "Auto Dealer Breaks Language Barriers to Lure Immigrants." LAT 8/3/87, IV:1

Bradsher, Keith, Maria L. La Ganga & Jesus Sanchez. "Pinatas and Pointsettias: Ethnic Stores, Restaurants See Holiday Business Surge." LAT 12/20/87, IV:1.

Braun, Stephan. "Learning the Ins and Outs of Driving." LAT 10/19/87, I:1

"Dallas Tops in Asian Businesses." LAHE 8/3/88, A-10

Easton, Nina J. "Japanese Firm in $100 Million Hollywood Deal." LAT 8/21/89, VI:1.

Frantz, Douglas. "Great Japanese Land Rush." LAT 3/8/89, IV:1.

Furlong, Tom. "Growing Influence of Asians on California Real Estate." LAT 8/14/88, IV:1.

Groves, Martha. "Boys Finds Niche in Urban Market." LAT 10/5/87, IV:1.

Harris, Scott. "Shades of Summer." LAT 7/14/89, II:1.

Hubler, Shawn. "Culture Shock Back Home for 'Americanized' Japanese." LAHE 5/13/88, A1.

Johnson, Greg. "More Firms Using Foreigners to Fill Professional Ranks." LAT 5/10/88, IV:1

Korean Directory of Southern California, Los Angeles: Keys Advertising and Printing Company, 1986.

Kotkin, Joel and Yoriko Kishimoto. "The Japanese are Banking on Los Angeles." LAT Magazine, 7/26/87:16.

La Guire, Lennie. "Americans Getting Oriented to Japanese Way of Business." LAHE 5/24/88, A1.

La Guire, Lennie. "Business Beckons to Korean Immigrants." LAHE 5/9/88, A1.

La Guire, Lennie and Shawn Hubler. "Many minorities add up to major new cultural force." LAHE 5/6/88, A1.

Light, Ivan. "Immigrant Entrepreneurs in America: Koreans in Los Angeles." In: Clamor at the Gates: The New American Immigration. Nathan J. Glazer, ed. San Francisco, ICS Press, 1985.

Lozano, Carlos V. "Entrepreneurs Get the Word Out on Ethnic Greeting Cards." LAT 12/24/87, W:4

"MEMO: Minority Car Dealers". LAT 4/4/88, IV:5.

Nineteen eighty-eight Japanese investment in United States Real Estate. Kenneth Leventhal and Company.

Nordwind, Richard. "Cornering of L.A.'s Markets." LAHE 6/28/87, A1

Oswald, John A. "China Busy Setting Up Shop." LAT 7/13/88, II:1.

Pristin, Terry and Eric Malnic. "Japanese Buy Hotel Bel-Air for $100 Million." LAT 5/2/89, I:1.

Rabin, Jeffrey, L. "Secretive Foreign Investors May Buy 49.9% of Marina del Rey Leasehold." LAT 7/30/89, IX:1.

Ryon, Ruth. "Brokers Flocking to Japan to Pitch U.S. Real Estate." LAT 6/12/88, VIII:1.

Sanchez, Jesus. "Population Growth Fueling Southland's Latino Business Boom." 9/28/87, IV:1.

Sanchez, Jesus. "Mini-Malls: Stores of Opportunity." LAT 9/20/87, IV:1.

Sanchez, Jesus. "L.A. Top Choice for Koreans in Business in U.S." LAT 6/6/87, IV:1.

Schacter, Jim and Nancy Yoshihara. "Bosses from Japan Bring Alien Habits." LAT 7/10/88, I:1.

Turpin, Dick. "Foreigners See L.A. Center as 'Mark of Leader' ". LAT 3/13/88, VIII:1.

Unger, Henry. "Asian Banks in U.S. Bow to Tradition." LAHE 2/22/88, D5.

Venant, Elizabeth. "L.A. Celebration Features Diverse Look at the Arts." LAT 9/20/88, VI:1.

Williams, Linda. "Language, the Key: Fluency in Many Tongues Can Unlock Sales for Southland Real Estate Agents." LAT 5/9/88, IV:1

Williams, Linda. "Talks set Scene for deals with Chinese Firms." LAT 5/28/88, IV:1.

Politics

Page 47   Ruben Casteneda

Page 48   Laurie Becklund

Becklund, Laurie. "300 Latino Leaders at Academic Conference Target Agenda of the '90s." LAT 10/29/88, II:1.

Boyarsky, Bill. "U.S. Pressures Board of Supervisors to Remap for Latino Representation." LAT 6/7/88.II:1.

Boyarsky, Bill. "Ethnic Politics Call for Deft Handling of Diverse Interests." LAT 1/29/89, II:1.

"Breaking Political Barriers and Stereotypes." LAHE 5/22/88, A1.

Brooks, Nancy Rivera. "Big Shift Among Ethnic Groups Seen by 1995." LAT 1/27/88, IV:2.

Casteneda, Ruben. "MALDEF Claims Racial Bias Against Hispanics." LAHE 9/22/88, A8.

Clayton, Janet. "Tenuous New Alliances Forged to Ease Korean-Black Tensions." LAT 7/20/87, II:1.

Connell, Rich. "Bradley Comes Under Pressure to Name Latinos to Top City Jobs." LAT 8/12/88, II:1.

Davis, Kevin. "81% of Naturalized Latinos Sign Up To Vote, Study Says." LAT 9/8/89, I:27.

Hernandez, Marita. "Tale of 2 Cultures." LAT 5/18/86, II:1.

Hudson, Berkeley. "Melting Pot Under a Microscope: UCLA Researchers Examine Changes in Monterey Park." LAT 10/23/88, W13.

Ito, Sheldon. "Culver City's Rising Ethnic Groups Seek Share of Clout." LAT 7/10/88, X:1.

Martinez, Richard and Antonio Gonzalez. "Latinos Should 'Take the Power.'" LAT 8/4/89, II:5.

Merina, Victor. Blacks Seek Role with Latinos in Redistributing Case." LAT 1/24/89,II:1.

Merina, Victor. "Latinos Open Fund Drive for County Bias Lawsuit." LAT 12/15/89, II:3.

Murphy, Kim. "Ruling Cites Bias Against Latino Voters." LAT 7/28/88, I:1.

Rogers, David. "Diversity of U.S. Asian Vote Presents Parties With Courtship Challenges and Opportunities." *Wall Street Journal*. 6/1/88,50.

Salholz, Eloise et. al. "A Conflict of the Have-Nots." *Newsweek*, 12/12/88:28–9.

Simon, Richard. "Future Uncertain for New Council Remap Plan." LAT 9/3/86, II:1.

Uranga, Steve and Marshall Diaz. "For Latinos, A Representative Case." 7/28/88, II:7.

Woo, Michael. Interview, 8/8/88.

Michael J. Ybarra. "More Latino Immigrants Seeking U.S. Citizenship." LAT 2/13/89, I:1.

Hispanic

Page 53   Julia Leiblich
Page 56   Garry Abrams
Page 56   Marc Haefele
Page 56   David L. Clark, p. 171
Page 57   Carey McWilliams, p. 52
Page 57   John D. Weaver, p. 148
Page 60   Rex Weiner
Page 62   James Loucky, p. 8

Abrams, Garry. "UCLA Extension Hears the Sound of *Musica* in Attracting Latinos." LAT 4/2/87, V:1.

Acuna, Rodolfo, F. *A Community Under Seige: A Chronicle of Chicanos East of the Los Angeles River, 1945–1975.* Los Angeles: UCLA, Chicano Studies Research Center, Monograph No. 11.

Acuna, Rudolfo. "Olvera Street Faces Wholesale Changes." LAHE 8/7/87,A19.

Argentine Cousulate Newsletter. March, 1988.

Auerbach, Susan. *Cityroots Festival: A Celebration of New Immigrant Traditions.* City of Los Angeles Cultural Affairs Department. 1987.

Beyette, Beverly. "It was a Short Hop from Havana." LAT 9/4/87, V:2.

Patricia Ward Biederman. "Blacks and Latinos Lag in Readiness for College." LAT 10/23/88, II:1.

Boudreau, Richard. "Nicaraguans Leaving in Droves as Economy Sinks." LAT 11/20/88, I:1.

Candel, Susan. Interview 11/17/88.

Castillo, Richard Griswald del. *The Los Angeles Barrio, 1850–1890.* Berkeley, Los Angeles, London: University of California Press, 1979.

Chavez, Stephanie and James Quinn. " Garages: Immigrants In, Cars Out." LAT 5/24/87, I:1.

Chilean Consulate. Telephone Interview, 9/8/87.

Clark, David L. *Los Angeles: A City Apart.* Woodland Hills, CA: Windsor Publications, 1981.

Crane, Tricia. "Return to the Good Old Days of the Dead." LAHE 10/30/87, Weekend Magazine.

Crittendon, Ann. "The Salvadorans Among Us Must be Helped" LAHE 10/3/88, A11.

Cummings, Judith. "The World of the Immigrant: Low-Paying Jobs and Overcrowded Housing." *New York Times* 4/13/87:6.

Directory of the Hispanic Community of the County of Los Angeles, (4th edition). USC Office of Hispanic Programs, College of Letters, Arts and Sciences. Office of Civic and Community Relations.

Doheny, Kathleen. "Bless 'Em All." LAT 4/2/88, V:1.

Drake, Joan. "*Olé* and Away they go for *Las Fiestas Patrias.* LAT 9/10/88, V:1.

Ecuadorean Consulate. Telephone Interview, 9/10/87.

Garcia, Ricardo (El Rescate). Telephone Interview, 11/16/88.

Guatamalan Information Center. Telephone Interview, 11/29/88.

Gompertz, Rolf. "Strangers in a Strange Culture." *KCET Magazine* 1/88, 1:1:52–55.

Haefele, Marc. "Forest Lawn Museum Resurrects Mexico Before the Conquest." LAT 8/6/87, V:F16.

Hendrix, Kathleen. " Center Offers Shelter From the Storm." LAT 12/10/87, V-A:1.

Kaplan, Tracey. "Dietary and Other Miracles Keep Animals on a Holy Path." LAT 4/3/88, I:28.

Hernandez, Marita. "Chicano Studies Finds Favor on Campus." LAT 4/10/89,I:3.

Hernandez, Marita. "Feeling at Home." LAT 8/19/89, II:1.

Horovitz, Bruce. "Spanish-Language Ads Are Catching On With Agencies in Southland." LAT 3/1/88,IV:1.

Horovitz, Bruce. "Disneyland Ads Aim for Latino Families." LAT 3/1/88, IV:1.

Leiblich, Julia. "If you Want a Big New Market. . . . " *Fortune*, 11/21/88.

Loucky, James. "Maya Migrants and Musical Traditions in Los Angeles." In Auerbach, 1987.

McCarthy, Kevin F. and R. Burciaga Valdez. *Current and Future Effects of Mexican Immigration in California: Executive Summary*. Santa Monica: The Rand Corporation, November 1985.

McWilliams, Carey. *Southern California: An Island on the Land*. 1983. Salt Lake City: Peregrine Smith. (First published 1946).

Melinkoff, Ellen "L.A. *Posadas*: A Tradition of Mexico." LAT 12/17/88, V:13.

Melinkoff, Ellen. "Expatriates Exhuberance Flavors L.A.'s Carnaval." LAT 2/4/89, V:16.

Melinkoff, Ellen. "Mexican Fete of Freedom This Weekend." LAT 9/12/87, V:4

Melinkoff, Ellen. "Pet Parade on Olvera Street." 4/18/87. IV:4.

Mitchell, Sean. "The Voice of L.A. Hispanics." LAHE 10/5/86, II:1.

Moffet, Penelope. "Latin Carnaval Atmosphere Fills Streets of Long Beach." LAT 5/21/88, V:1.

Newton, Edmund & Jill Stewart. "Cinco de Mayo, Los Angeles Style: Fun, Food and a Lesson in History." LAT 5/4/87, II:1

Newton, Edmund. "East L.A. Latinos Show Pride in Colorful Heritage." LAT 9/14/87, II:3.

O'Donnell, Santiago. "L.A.'s Cubans Ambivalent and Cautious About Prison Revolt." LAT 12/3/87, II:1.

O'Shaughnessy, Lynn. "Independence Day: Mexican Pride on Parade." LAT 9/15/86, V:1

Parachini, Allan. "Latinos in California: A Cultural Heritage in Search of a Museum." LAT 1/17/88, VI:1.

"Pet Parade on Olvera Street." LAT 4/18/87, IV:4.

Rand, Christopher. *Los Angeles: The Ultimate City*. NY: Oxford University Press, 1967.

Rodriguez, Richard. "Success Stories: Voices from an Emerging Elite." LAT Magazine 11/6/88:8.

Sanchez, Jesus. "Ex-Produce Clerk Leads Vons Toward the Latino Market." LAT 8/31/87, IV:1.

Seale, Jim. "Latino Holiday for the Dead is Alive in L.A." LAT 10/29/87, V:4

Simon, Richard and Stephanie Chavez. "Upwardly Mobile Latinos Shift Their Political Views." LAT 12/26/87, II:1.

Thompson, Ginger Lynne. "Mexican Independence Fest Draws 100,000 to East L.A." LAT 9/12/88, II:1.

Tobar, Hector. "Salvadoran Loyalties Clash in L.A." LAT 2/12/89, I:1.

Valdez, R.Burciaga " A Framework for Policy development for the Latino Population: Testimony Before the California Hispanic Legislative Conference." Santa Monica: The Rand Corporation, P 7207, April 1986.

Weaver, John D. *El Pueblo Grande*. 1973. Los Angeles: The Ward Ritchie Press.

Weiner, Rex. "La Boylé." LAT Magazine 6/18/89:18.

Weisman, Alan. "Born in East L.A." LAT Magazine, 3/27/88, 11–25.

Asian

Page 69   Shawn Hubler, LAHE 5/25/88

Page 69   Mark Arax, LAT Magazine, 12/13/87

Page 70   Carol McGraw

Page 71   Mark Arax, LAT 4/5/87

Page 72   David L. Clark, p.160

Page 73   P.W. Dooner, p.21

Page 74   Charles Choy Wong, p.71

Page 76   Ashley Dunn, LAT 9/8/88

Page 77   Edmund Newton

Page 77   Claudia Puig

Page 79   Adrianne Goodman

Page 81   Sam Hall Kaplan

Page 81   Siok-Hian Tay Kelley

Page 83   Kenneth J. Garcia, LAT 5/24/88

Page 85   Nolan Zane et.al., p.53

Page 85   Herminia Menez and Susan Montepio, p.12

Page 87   Kenneth J. Garcia, LAT 3/25/88

Page 91   Scott Ostler

Page 93   Mary Lou Fulton

Page 93   Amy Catlin, p.31

Aoki, Guy. "All-Asian Radio Set to Debut in November." LAT 9/5/88, VI:1. USC Dissertation, 1952.

Aquino, Valentin R. "The Filipino Community in Los Angeles." USC Dissertation, 1952.

Arax, Mark. "Group Seeks to Reverse Voter Apathy by Asians." LAT 3/3/86, II:1.

Arax, Mark. "Asian Influx Alters Life in Suburbia." LAT 4/5/87, I:1.

Arax, Mark. "Nation's First Suburban Chinatown." LAT 4/6/87, I:1.

Arax, Mark. "Lost in L.A." LAT Magazine 12/13/87, I:1.

Arax, Mark. "Cambodians in L.A. Area Flee Fearing Quake." LAT 5/20/88, I:1.

Arax, Mark. "Pooled Cash of Loan Clubs Key to Asian Immigrant Enterpreneurs." LAT 10/30/88, II:1.

Auerbach, Susan. *Cityroots Festival: A Celebration of New Immigrant Traditions*. City of Los Angeles Cultural Affairs Department, 1987.

Baker, Chris. "Carson's Samoan Connection Creates Problem." LAT 9/23/80, III:5.

Blume, Howard. "A Rite of Passage." LAT 12/16/88. II:3.

Braun, Stephen. "For Asians, A Ritual Sip of Home." LAT 2/16/89, I:1.

"Breaking Political Barriers and Stereotypes." LAHE 5/22/88, A1.

Casteneda, Ruben. "Poor English Skills Almost Keep Needed Cops off the Street." LAHE 12/11/88.

Catlin, Amy. "The Vo Family: Vietnamese Musicians, Singing Actresses and Ritual Performers." In Auerbach, 1987.

Catlin, Amy and Dixie Swift. *Textiles as Texts: Arts of Hmong Women from Laos*, 1987.

Churm, Steven R. "Little India." LAT 4/6/86, II:1.

Clark, David L. *Los Angeles: A City Apart*. Woodland Hills, CA: Windsor Publications, 1981.

College of Buddhist Studies, Schedule of Classes, 8/87.

Daniels, Roger. *Asian America: Chinese and Japanese in the United States since 1850*." Seattle: University of Washington Press, 1988.

Dart, John. "2 Americans Elected Vice Presidents of Buddhist Organization." LAT 11/25/88, II:1.

Dart, John. "Buddhism reaches Out in America." LAT 11/20/88, II:1.

De Wolfe, Evelyn. "Hotel Slated in Little Tokyo." LAT 7/17/88, VIII:1.

Devoss, David. "Oasis for L.A.'s Viet Buddhists." LAT 10/20/87, V:1.

Dooner, P.W. *Last Days of the Republic*. San Francisco: Alta California Publishing House. 1800.

Downey, Mike. "A Slice of Seoul in L.A." LAT 9/14/88,III:1.

Du Brow, Rick. "KSCI's the Voice from home for Local Asians." LAHE 5/21/88, C1.

Dunn, Ashley. "Advice Column Focuses on Chinese Immigrants." LAT 9/8/88, W14.

Dunn, Ashley. "East Meets East." LAT 5/27/89, II:1.

Dunn, Ashley. "For Some Chinese Living by the Numbers is Safest." LAT 5/28/89. I:1.

Estapa, Andrea. "First Korean Float Brings Pride to Growing Community." LAT 1/2/88, I:2.

Faris, Gerald. "Designer Planted Seeds of Fashion in Japanese Community." LAT 9/29/88,W:13.

Feldman, Paul. "A Taste of Old Japan in New Year Rite." LAT 12/29/88, II:3.

Frantz, Douglas. "Great Japanese Land Rush." LAT 3/8/89, IV:1.

Fulton, Mary Lou. "Shrine Sculpted from a Dream." LAT 10/14/88: II:3

Furlong, Tom. "Growing Influence of Asians on California Real Estate." LAT 8/14/88, IV:1

Garcia, Kenneth J. "A Shot in the Rough." LAT 5/24/88, II:3.

Garcia, Kenneth J. "Sight to Behold." LAT 3/25/88, II:1.

Goodman, Adrianne. "Institute Perpetuates Japanese Culture." LAT 9/1/88, W:10.

Gordon, Larry. "Universities Feeling pull of Far East." LAT 11/7/88, I:1.

Haldane, David. "Asian Girls: A Cultural Tug of War." LAT 9/24/88, I:1

Haldane, David. "Culture Clash or Animal Cruelty?" LAT 3/13/89, II:1.

Haldane, David. "Buddhist Center Offers Slice of Home to Cambodian Refugees." LAT 8/7/88, W10.

Haldane, Davis. "Cambodian Buddhists Keep Faith in Unobtrusive Suburban Temple." LAT 8/27/87, W14.

Haldane, David. "A Taste of Cambodia." LAT 12/19/88, IV:1.

Hansen, Barbara. "L.A.'s Passage to India." LAT Magazine, 10/1/89:28.

Harris, Scott. "Plan for Little Tokyo Development Gains." LAT 1/20/88, II:1.

Henstell, Bruce. *Sunshine and Wealth: Los Angeles in the Twenties and Thirties.* San Francisco: Chronicle, 1984.

Hill, Nancy Jo. "Festivities Herald Chinese New Year." LAT 2/18/89, V:17.

Hirabayashi, Lane Ryo and George Tanaka. "The Issei Community in Moneta and the Gardena Valley, 1900–1920. *Southern California Quarterly*, Summer 1988, V.LXX, #2:127 -57.

Holley, David. "Little Tokyo Festival Forges East-West Link." LAT 8/9/86, II:1.

Holley, David. "Refugees build a Haven in Long Beach." LAT 10/27/86, II:1.

Hubler, Shawn. "Filipino Town: Big Enough for Both Sides?" LAHE 5/10/88, A1.

Hubler, Shawn. "Indian Women Say 'I don't' to Marriage at First Sight," LAHE 5/11/88, A1.

Hubler, Shawn. "The Vietnam War was *Their* War—and They're still Fighting It." LAHE 5/15/88, A1.

Hubler, Shawn. "Golf Industry a Matter of Course for Driven Japanese Businessmen." LAHE 5/19/88, A1.

Hubler, Shawn. "Samoan Youth Fight Poverty and 'Beast of Burden' Image." LAHE 5/20/88, A1.

Hubler, Shawn. "Fear of Failing Makes Students Testy." LAHE 5/25/88, A1.

Hubler, Shawn. "Thai Community Insider is a Virtue on the Vice Squad." LAHE 5/26/88, A:1

Hudson, Berkeley. "Melting Pot under a Microscope: UCLA Researchers Examine Change in Monterey Park." LAT 10/23/88, W13.

Hudson, Berkeley. "Ancient Asian Game Could Go Far as Americans Catch On." LAT 2/12/89, II:1.

Hudson, Berkeley. "Monterey Park, Star 'Melting Pot,' Getting Fed Up with Publicity." LAT 4/6/89, W:5.

Kaeonil, Narong. "The Thai Community in Los Angeles: An Attitudinal Study of its Socio-Economic Structure." Ph.D. 1977, United States International University.

Kaplan, Sam Hall. "New Japanese Pavilion is Work of Art Itself." LAT Calendar, 10/25/88:6.

Kelley, Siok-Hian Tay. "Wives of Visiting Japanese Execs Discover Simple Pleasures." LAT 10/13/88, W:11.

Korean Directory of Southern California, 1986–7. Los Angeles: Keys Ad and Printing Company, 1986.

Kotkin, Joel and Yoriko Kishimoto. "The Japanese are Banking on Los Angeles." LAT Magazine, 7/26/87:16.

"L.A. Facts" LAHE 8/3/88, A9.

La Guire, Lennie and Shawn Hubler. "Many minorities add up to major new cultural force." LAHE 5/6/88, A1.

La Guire, Lennie. "Business Beckons to Korean Immigrants." LAHE 5/9/88, A1.

La Guire, Lennie. "A One-Generation Chinese Family." LAHE 5/12/88, A1.

La Guire, Lennie. "American Zen Practioners out-Korean the Koreans." LAHE 5/14/88, A1.

La Guire, Lennie. "Chinese Tradition Divides Mother, Daughter." LAHE 5/18/88, A1.

La Guire, Lennie. "Americans Getting Oriented to Japanese Way of Business." LAHE 5/24/88, A1.

Larsen, David. "Honor Thy Parents." LAT 10/23/88, VI:1.

LAT "The Olympics 'Return' to Los Angeles." 9/11/88, II:1

Lewis, Jennifer. "Study Shows 'untold need' in Asian Pacific Community. LAHE 7/28/88, A8.

Light, Ivan. "Immigrant Enterpreneurs in America: Koreans in Los Angeles." In: *Clamor at the Gates: The New American Immigration*, Nathan J. Glazer, ed. San Francisco: ICS Press, 1985:161–78.

Mason, William M. and John A. McKinstry. *The Japanese of Los Angeles*. Los Angeles: Los Angeles County Museum, 1969.

McGraw, Carol. " 'Untold Human Need' Found in Asian Community." LAT 7/28/88,II:1.

McMillan, Penelope. "Chinese Cultural Center a Step Closer to Reality." LAT 6/4/88, II:3.

McMillan, Penelope. "Chinatown: A Way of Life." LAT 6/26/88, II:1.

Menez, Herminia and Susan Montepio. "The *Santacruzan* Festival in the Filipino Community of Los Angeles." In Auerbach, 1987.

Newton, Edmund. "East Settling into West." LAT 1/10/88, II:1.

Njeri, Itabari. "Prom Night." LAT 6/7/87, VI:1.

Njeri, Itabari. "Herbalists's Ancient Remedies Can Rattle Your Composure." LAT 10/29/87, V:1.

Njeri, Itabari. "Buddhist Goes with the Odds." LAT 1/20/88, V:1.

Njeri, Itabari. "The Turning Point." LAT 1/1/89, VI:1.

Ostler, Scott. "Carson's Samoan Connection: 20 on One Football Team." LAT 12/16/78, III:1.

Peterson, Jonathan. "Filipinos—A Search for Community." LAT 5/24/89, I:1.

Pierson, Robert John. "Chinatown." LAT 2/14/89, V:16.

Puig, Claudia. "Year of the Dragon." LAT 2/14/88, II:1.

Rao, Nalini. Interview, 5/26/88.

Rosenstiel, Thomas B. "L.A. Papers Speak a New Language." LAT 11/9/87, I:1.

Sanchez, Jesus. "Dishing Up the Ramen." LAT 2/8/88, IV:1.

Sanchez, Jesus. "L.A. Top Choice for Koreans in Business in U.S." LAT 6/6/87, IV:1.

Santoli, Al. "Mrs. Noup's Life Before Donuts." *L.A. Reader*, 12/9/88:1.

Schifrin, Matthew. "Horatio Alger Kim." *Forbes*, 10/17/88:92 -6.

Schwartz, John et.al. "Tapping into a Blossoming Asian Market." *Newsweek* 9/7/87, W:12.

Searles, Jack. "East Meets West." LAHE 8/3/86, E1.

Spano, John. "Chinatown Seniors in Housing Protest March." LAT 9/28/88, II:1

Stevens, Amy. "Couples Together Again" LAT 6/11/88, II:1.

Tagashira, Gail S. "A Spirited Dance." LAT 7/23/88, V:1.

Thompson, Ginger Lynn. "State Asians, Pacific Islanders Face Hostility, Panel Tells Van de Kamp." LAT 1/7/89. I:24.

Venant, Elizabeth. "L.A. Celebration Features Diverse Look at the Arts." LAT 9/20/88, VI:1.

Weber, Bruce. "Nirvana Deluxe in Lotus Land." *New York Times Magazine* 8/4/88, section 6.

Williams, Linda. "Talks Set Scene for Deals with Chinese Firms." LAT 5/28/88, IV:1.

Wong, Charles Choy. "Ethnicity, Work and Community: The Case of Chinese in Los Angeles." Ph.D., UCLA, 1979.

Woo, Michael. Interview, 8/8/88.

Yamada, Kenneth T. "Japanese Couples Discover L.A. as Place to Tie Knot." LAT 8/27/88, II:3.

Ybarra, Michale J. "Rapidly growing Korean Community Looks at its Problems, Its Future."LAT 12/11/88, II:1.

Yoshihara, Nancy. "Koreatown Embarks on a New Phase." LAT 12/28/87, IV:5.

Zane, Nolan, et. al. *United Way Asian Pacific Needs Assessment Technical Report.* Los Angeles, July 1988.

European

Page 98   Laurance L. Hill, p.98

Page 98   W.W. Robinson, section 25

Page 102   Sam Hall Kaplan

Baskauskas, Liucija. *An Urban Enclave: Lithuanian Refugees in Los Angeles.* New York: AMS Press, 1985.

British Consulate. Telephone Interview, 9/10/87.

Caughey, John and LaRee. *Los Angeles: Biography of a City.* Berkeley, 1974.

Chazonov, Mathis. "Soviet Jews to Get Help Relocating in Los Angeles." LAT 1/15/89, 14:1.

Chazonov, Mathis and Esther Schrader. "Southland Not Prepared for Soviet Emigrees." LAT 2/19/89, 14:1.

Clark, David L. *Los Angeles: A City Apart.* Woodland Hills, CA: Windsor Publications, 1981.

Crocken, Maria (German Consulate). Telephone Interview 9/10/87.

Dean, Paul. "Gypsies are Banding Together to Fight Age-Old Stereotypes." LAT 10/5/86, VI:1.

Fay, Laura (Irish Network). Telephone Interview, 9/2/89.

Gold, Steven J. "New Immigrants and Ethnic Solidarity: The Case of the Soviet Jews in California." Immigration Research Program Lecture Series, 11/10/88.

Gordon, Larry. "Scents, Sounds of Italy Fill Los Feliz Air." LAT 12/21/86, W:6.

Greek Heritage Society of America. Telephone Interview, 11/22/88.

Greene, Bob. "It's not all Just Greek to Them." LAHE 5/24/88:B1

Gribben, Arthur and Maesha Maguire (compilers). *The Irish Cultural Directory for Southern California.* Los Angeles: UCLA Folklore Mythology Publications, 1985.

Hill, Laurance L. *La Reina: Los Angeles in Three Centuries*, Los Angeles: Security Trust and Savings Bank, 1929.

Kaplan, Sam Hall. " A Fresh Start for Rodia's Watts Towers." LAT 6/11/88, V:4.

Karhuvaara, Pekka (Finnish Consulate). Telephone Interview, 8/26/87.

Laan, Bruno (Estonian House). Telephone Interview, 9/18/89.

Luxembourg Consulate. Telephone Interview, 8/24/87.

Matich, Olga. Interview, 1/20/88.

McLoughlin, Robert (Irish Fair). Telephone Interview, 9/2/89.

McWilliams, Carey. *Southern California: An Island on the Land.* Salt Lake City: Peregrine Smith, 1983. (First published 1946).

Parks, Michael. "Soviet Emigrees to U.S. in '89 May Hit 60,000." LAT 1/3/89, I:1.

Pyrillis, Rita. "Little Bit of Holland is Mostly Memories." LAT 4/26/87, II:1.

Reins, Alfons C. (Latvian Association of Southern California). Telephone Interview, 9/19/89.

Robinson, W.W. *Panorama: A Picture History of Southern California* Los Angeles, 1953.

Sandburg, Neil. *Ethnic Identity and Assimilation: The Polish-American Community Case Study of Metropolitan Los Angeles*, 1972.

Stein, Jeannine. "Pomp and Circumstance of Nobility Among Us." LAT 6/8/86, VI:1.

Swedish Consulate. Telephone Interview, 9/22/87.

Thompson, Ginger Lynn. "Glasnost, California Style." LAT 11/6/88, W1.

Weaver, John D. *Los Angeles: The Enormous Village 1781–1981.* Santa Barbara, 1981.

Welzenbach, Michael. "Annual Scottish Festival at Costa Mesa." LAT 5/28/88, V:1.

Willard, Charles Dwight. *The Herald's History of Los Angeles City.* Los Angeles: Kingsley, Baines and Neuner, Co. 1901.

Middle East

Page 115   David Weddle

Aivazian, Gia. Interview 1/8/88.

Albert, Elaine (Commission on Israelis). Telephone Interview, 9/1/89.

Al-Marayati, Salam (Councilman Robert Farrell's Office). Telephone Interview, 8/12/88.

Arax, Mark and Esther Schrader. "Armenians Find Refuge in Hollywood." LAT 4/25/88, I:1.

Armenian Directory. Southern California: Uniarts, 1987.

Auerbach, Susan. *Cityroots Festival: A Celebration of New Immigrant Traditions.* City of Los Angeles Cultural Affairs Department, 1987.

Beauchamp, Marc. "Welcome to Teheran, Calif." *Forbes* 12/12/88:60.

Beyette, Beverly. "His Majesty, the Exile." LAT 10/3/88, V:1.

Choppin, Rachel. Telephone Interview, 8/29/89.

Chazanov, Mathis. "Southland Bahai Faithful Dedicate New L.A. Center." LAT 9/12/88, II:1.

Cano, Mrs. Suad (Founder, Arab Community Center). Telephone Interview, 12/2/88.

Haiek, Joseph, R. ed. *Arab American Almanac*, third edition. Glendale: The News Circle Publishing Co., 1984.

"L.A. Help for Armenian Refugees Urged." LAT 8/26/88, II:3.

Light, Ivan, Georges Sabagh and Mehdi Bozorgmehr. Report of ongoing UCLA study on Muslim Iranis, 5/18/88.

Manjikian, Tamar. "Sustaining the Armenian Quake Relief Effort." LAT 1/15/89, VI:4.

McCarley, William R. "City's role in Resettlement of Soviet Armenian Refugees." City of Los Angeles Memorandum, 7/1/88.

Murphy, Dean. "Armenian Group, Residents go Back to Table." LAT 2/25/88, W3.

Nazario, Sonia L. "Soviet Armenians Find New Foe Here: Their Countrymen," *Wall Street Journal* 3/3/89:1.

Roderick, Kevin. "Pain of Loss Helps to heal Armenian Rift." LAT 12/12/88, I:1.

Sass, Stephen, J. ed. *Jewish Los Angeles: A Guide*. 2nd edition. Jewish Federation Council of Greater Los Angeles, 1982.

Schrader, Esther. "Inner Dispute Clouds Future for Armenian Emigre Ranks." LAT 7/10/88, II:1.

Schrader, Esther. "Arriving Armenians Face Tighter Rules, Less Government Aid." LAT 9/2/88, II:3.

Schrader, Esther and Doug Smith. "L.A. Armenians Mobilize to Aid Victims." LAT 12//9/88, I:13.

"3,000 Attend Armenian Festival." LAT 10/10/88.

Weddle, David. "L.A.'s Palestinians: Twice victimized?" L.A. *Weekly* 8/14–20/87:22.

African

Page 117–8   Asante Cultural Society News Release
Page 119   Iris Schneider

Asante Cultural Society News Release, 1/88.

Brooks, H. Dennis. "Garifuna Community Celebrate Settlement Day '88. *Community Voice: A Focus on the Belize and Caribbean Community*. Vol.1, No. 1, Nov-Dec. 1988.

Harris, Scott. "Religious Groups Fear Animal Protection Law would Stifle Rituals." LAT 8/8/88, II:1.

Kenyan Consulate. Telephone Interview, 8/17/87.

Libman, Gary. "Modern Kwanzaa Festival Honors the Black Heritage." LAT 12/24/88, V:14.

Mitchell, Rick. "Power of the *Orishas*." LAT Magazine 2/7/88:16.

Mayi, Aliyu. Interview, 5/1/88.

Nana Osei Tutu Appiah. Interview, 5/4/88.

Oswald, John A. "Ethiopian Keeps Lonely Vigil Helping Countrymen Settle in U.S." LAT 8/1/88, II:1.

Rosen, Dan. "Sect Stands up for its Rites-the Sacrifice of Animals." LAHE 8/9/88, A3.

Schneider, Iris. "Marketplace: A Bit of Africa Every Month." LAT 8/21/88, II:5.

Simross, Lynn. "Kwanzaa Week Celebrates Rich Black Heritage." LAT 12/26/87, IV:1.

Teitelbaum, Sheldon. "A Marketplace of African Authenticity." LAT 8/19/89, IV:15.

Turk, Rose-Marie. "Hip Garb has a Deep-Rooted Appeal." LAT 8/25/89, V:1.

Los Angeles Tomorrow

Page 136   Itabari Njeri

"America Learns to Love L.A." *The Economist*, London, 12/24- 1/6,88–89.

Hayes-Bautista, David E. *The Burden of Support: Young Latinos in an Aging Society*. Stanford University Press, 1988.

L.A.2000: Final report of the Los Angeles 2000 Committee. Submitted to The Honorable Tom Bradley, 11/15/88.

Njeri, Itabari. "The Melting Pot Myth." LAT 11/2/88. V:1.

Oliver, Myrna. "Cultural Defense—A Legal Tactic." LAT 7/15/88, I:1.

Reuben, Liz. "Ratio of Asians Will Grow Fastest." LAHE 9/13/89, A1.

Wolpert, Stuart. "A Tale of Two Cities." *UCLA Magazine*, 1(1):60–5. Spring 1989.

Wong, May. "Professor Says Californians Should Be Looking to Future." *Daily Bruin* 5/17/88:13.

UNITED STATES MIGRANTS

Page 125   Lynn Simross

Page 126   Brian Eisleben, p.7

Page 127   Guy Maxtone-Graham

Page 128   Mary Ellen Strote

Page 128   Lonnie G. Bunch III, pp.24–25

Page 129   Beth Miller

Page 130   David L. Clark, p.170

Page 131   Bob Baker

Page 132   Kimberly L. Jackson and Lucille Renwick

Afro-American Resource Center Leaflet.

Baker, Bob. "View Park." LAT 8/25/86, II:1.

Boyarsky, Bill. "1st Step in Watts Redevelopment Taken." LAT 8/25/88, I:1.

Bunch, Lonnie G. III. *Black Angelenos: The Afro-American in Los Angeles, 1850–1950*. Los Angeles: California Afro-American Museum, 1988.

Citron, Alan. "Aging Indians Finding They Can Go Home Again." LAT 3/6/88, I:1.

Clark, David L. *Los Angeles; A City Apart*. Woodland Hills, CA: Windsor Publications, 1981.

Eisleben, Brian. "Indian Resource Center: Serving L.A.'s Native Americans." *Reader*, 3/27/87:7.

Hanson, Earl and Paul Beckett. *Los Angeles: Its People and its Homes*. Los Angeles: The Haynes Foundation, 1944.

Harris, Scott. "Ground Broken for Huge Housing Project in Watts." LAT 11/30/88, II:3.

Jackson, Kimberly, L. and Lucille Renwick. "Reunion Celebrates the Black Family and Offers Some Support." LAT 8/28/88, II:1.

Kalb, Ben and John Gottberg Anderson. "Southern California." APA Productions.

Kelley, Daryl. "Poorest South L.A. Areas Ticketed for Development." LAT 11/3/88, I:1.

Maxtone-Graham, Guy. "Indians to Meet at CSUN for Summit Conference." LAT 9/24/88, II:4.

McGarry, T.W. "Indian Feud: Development Brings Out the War Paint." LAT 6/4/88, II:1.

McMillan, Penelope. "The Urban Indian—L.A.'s Factionalized Minority." LAT 10/26/80, II:1.

McMillan, Penelope. "Black Flight from L.A. Reverses Trend, Study Discovers." LAT 9/22/87, II:1.

McMillan, Penelope. "Granddaughter Keeps Memory of Pioneering Black Journalist Vivid." LAT 9/5/88, II:1.

Miller, Beth. "A Trip Through Oakwood." *Free Venice Beachhead*, 7/88:7.

Njeri, Itabari. "St. Brigid Gets a Taste of That Old-Time Religion." LAT 5/17/87, VI:1.

Nordwind, Richard. "City on the Way Back." LAHE 4/5/87, A1.

Quintana. Craig. "Restored Hotel to be Symbol of Blacks' History." LAT 8/23/87, II:1.

Simross, Lynn. "The Plight of the Native Americans on the Urban Reservation.'" LAT 4/16/86, V:1.

Strote, Mary Ellen. "The Glories of Warriors." LAT 6/11/88, V:1.

"Urban Indians-Los Angeles." Notes, American Indian Resource Center, Huntington Park Library.

Weaver, John D. *Los Angeles: The Enormous Village, 1781–1981*. Santa Barbara, 1981.

Welkos, Robert. "Indians Cite Culture Loss, Seek Ban on Bogus Jewelry." LAT 9/26/88, II:1.

Woo, Elaine. "Fairfax High Students Stage Black Bias Protest." LAT 3/10/88, II:1.

Appendices

Boyden, Donald P. ed. *Gale Directory of Publications*, Vol.1, 121st edition. Detroit: Gale Research, Inc., 1989.

Burum, Linda and S. Irene Virbila. *Cook's Marketplace, Los Angeles*. San Francisco: 101 Productions, 1986.

Fister, Nancy (compiler). *Directory: Annual Multicultural Festivals in the Los Angeles Area*. Los Angeles: Cultural Affairs Department, 1988.

Rosenstiel, Thomas B. "L.A. Papers Speak a New Language." LAT 11/9/87, I:1.

Index

INDEX

Photography

Bradley International Terminal, Zena Pearlstone
Hsi Lai Temple, Courtesy Hsi Lai Temple
Business Signs, Jay T. Last and Zena Pearlstone
Vermont Avenue Mall, Jay T. Last
Public School Children, Rodney E. Raschke. "Copyright 1987 Rodney E. Raschke, all rights reserved."
City Hall, Copyright Rodney E. Raschke. "Copyright 1981 Rodney E. Raschke, all rights reserved."
The Plumed Serpent, Willie Herrón. "Copyright Willie Herrón."
Blessing of the Animals, Courtesy El Pueblo de Los Angeles Historic Park
Chinatown, Jay T. Last
Irish Pub, Zena Pearlstone
Saint Sophia, Courtesy Saint Sophia Greek Orthodox Cathedral
The Islamic Center, Rodney E. Raschke. "Copyright 1987 Rodney E. Raschke, all rights reserved."
Coronation, Rodney E. Raschke. "Copyright 1987 Rodney E. Raschke, all rights reserved."
African Marketplace, James Burks, William Grant Still Art Center
Australian Store, Zena Pearlstone
Watts Towers, Rodney E. Raschke. "Copyright 1975 Rodney E. Raschke, all rights reserved."
Newspapers, Jay T. Last and Zena Pearlstone
Japanese Drummers, Rodney E. Raschke. "Copyright 1987 Rodney E. Raschke, all rights reserved."
Sree Venkateswara Temple, Zena Pearlstone
Restaurant Signs, Jay T. Last and Zena Pearlstone

Design: Lilli Cristin
Typography: Andresen Typographics, Tucson
Lithography: Dai Nippon, Tokyo